PRAISE FOR LIVING

In *Living in the Different*, Reverend Sturtz sets us free to live, grieve, die and live again by pouring into us out of her experience, both deep and wide, as person, pastor, chaplain and friend. She offers what she knows in her head and heart with transparency and vulnerability.

Bishop Gregory V. Palmer
Resident Bishop of the West Ohio Conference
The United Methodist Church

After nearly fifty years as a Funeral Director and reading all I could to help families in their grief journey, Rev. Elaine Sturtz' own personal journey in and through grief is a must-read for every funeral director, hospice worker, physician and clergy person and especially for those suffering the death of a loved one. As she walks with you through her own grief, the death of her husband, her parents and friends, she will provide you with guidance, strength and understanding of the grief process, but most especially "Hope" through the scriptures. Every person who reads *Living in the Different* will be blessed by Rev. Sturtz' understanding and writings about this very complex thing called Grief. It has surely been a comfort and blessing to me.

Dwayne R. Spence, CFSP
Past President, Ohio Funeral Directors Assn.
Past President, National Funeral Directors Assn.

Living In The Different is a very real and raw look at how life changes when we lose those we love. Thank you, Rev. Elaine Sturtz for sharing your heart, your priceless experiences and your educated views on living, death, loss and survival of all of these journeys. We are all going to lose loved ones at some point in our life; although it is never easy, life goes on even when we want it to wait on us to catch up. Having been in hospice leadership for over fifteen years of my career, every death experience is different and personal for someone who loves that person! *Living in the Different* is a beautifully written book of experiences and advice that will benefit so many as they go through the journey of life and loss. It also does a brilliant job of reminding all of us of the Hope of a Hope!

Holly Franko
President, LHC Group
Hospice Division

Living in the Different is an insightful must-read of comfort and support for individuals seeking assistance through the difficult process of loss of a loved one. Rev. Elaine Sturtz has written an incredibly insightful guide through grief, based upon her decades of experience. As a Methodist Minister, Hospice Chaplain, and Grief Counselor, she shares her years of professional insights of the grieving process with the reader. Losing her own beloved husband, Rev. Sturtz shares her personal challenges of her own path to healing the hole in her heart and continuing to live her life without him by her side. This book is an honest and straightforward account based upon Rev. Sturtz's knowledgeable understanding of grief, recovery and living.

Mary L. Taylor RN, LNHA, Esquire

LIVING IN THE DIFFERENT

The passages through sorrow and loss

Elaine J. Clinger Sturtz

LIVING IN THE DIFFERENT

The passages through sorrow and loss

Elaine J. Clinger Sturtz

DECLARATION
PRESS

DECLARATION PRESS

Living in the Different:
The Passages Through Sorrow and Loss
Copyright © 2018 by Elaine J. Clinger Sturtz
All Rights Reserved

Photography: Chris Laner, LeAnne Gompf
Cover design: Steven Fisher

ISBN-13: 978-0-9983102-3-7

In Memory
of my Dear Husband, Dave.

You taught me what it means to love deeply,
how to enjoy life together,
how to walk the journey of dying with grace.
Through your life and through your death,
God walked beside us.
Love never ends.

God gave me comfort on the journey,
so that I could comfort others on the journey.

May these words bring you comfort.
May they be a guide on your journey.

CONTENTS

ACKNOWLEDGEMENTS

Thanks be to God for all those who came before me and those God put on my path to walk this pathway of sorrow and loss. I am thankful for all I have experienced on the journey.

Thank you to my editors and proofreaders—Becki Fogle, my sweet friend, and Merilyn Clinger, my dear aunt.

Thank you to Steve Fisher for the cover design. I recognized Steve's talent when he was in High School drawing coal trucks at work camp. Steve was a youth when I was a youth minister.

Thank you to Chris Laner and LeAnne Gompf for their beautiful photos that describe the journey that words cannot always explain.

Thank you to Denny Livingston and the Grief Class in Upper Sandusky for allowing me to share some of these writings and to refine them through the class.

Thank you to Mike and Sue Murphy for sharing their journey and finding a way to honor the memory of their son, Jason, who was one of my former youth.

Thank you, God, for walking me through my own sorrow and loss so that I may share my journey with those who follow me.

CHAPTER 1

INTRODUCTION

How deep is the mud? It depends on whom you ask and the viewpoint. How deep is the grief? It depends on whom you ask. We all go through sorrow and loss differently. Grief has common expressions for each loss, but each person who grieves the loss is different.

This book was created for all who are filled with sorrow. You have experienced the death of someone dear to you. I am so sorry for your loss. As you walk this uncharted path of grief and loss, may these words be a guide on your personal journey.

My words come from a heart that has been broken — a heart that felt the pain and loss of the most important person in my life but also found hope in the midst of grief and blessings in the memories.

We tend to live in two worlds in our grief — the world of grief and sorrow and the world of the present day. Our focus tends to be on the past — our loved one, the loss and the memories. The present seems too hard without our loved one. We retreat to the past in our hearts and minds while our bodies attempt to function in the present world.

My hope and prayer is that the words on these pages will assist your journey in this chapter of grief. The pages are filled with numerous struggles we face on the path— the emotions, the relationships, the last days, material memories, who we are, the changes, and movement into a new reality and a hope of a hope.

As a United Methodist Minister, a former hospice chaplain and a Licensed Professional Clinical Counselor (LPCC), I walked the journey with the dying and supported those who were grieving. I counseled those who were grieving and assisted them in finding a new life and path. I experienced the death of church family, my grandmother, my parents and dear friends and extended family. Then my husband of twenty-five and a half years died. My view and understanding of grief changed. I experienced the intensity of loss and loneliness. My world turned totally upside down and different.

I continued my counseling ministry shortly after my husband died, and God brought to my ministry many who were grieving intensely the loss of spouses, parents, children and friends. Counseling clients helped me work through my grief. I was *giving* support and comfort, and I *received* that comfort from God in return.

In looking at the past, I saw the faithfulness of God. God brought me through the valleys, the heartaches and hurts of my past. I had to trust Him in the present to see me through the grief and find meaning and purpose in the next chapter of my life.

As I started to write a book on the life lessons and fruits of labor of my husband's life, I realized I had a huge amount of grief stories within me. So, I began to write, but my writing took a different direction, and this book is the result. Then I began to teach a grief class in my hometown and to share these writings.

I have attempted to address some of the topics that I did not see addressed very often in what I had read. Grief is not neat and orderly. It does not follow defined stages and tasks, though they are included in our grief. Grief, to me, is messy, hard, and painful, filled with tears and loneliness, but it also includes faith, hope and love. Our love and sorrow are mingled together.

Grief feels like living in a snow globe. We are shaken up and turned upside down. Life settles for a moment, and then we are turned upside down without warning. Love never ends, and that is what sustains us through our grief. The love and the memories can never be taken from us.

Interspersed in these pages are personal stories and memories of those whom God placed on my path to walk both the road of dying and the road of grief. In our grief, we learn from the fruit of the lives that came before us — we learn about living and making a life matter. We learn about the legacy of love.

May these words give you comfort in your sorrow. May you experience the warmth of God's love and presence through these words. May you find a hope for a new chapter of your life. May your sorrow and love mingle together as you walk through this chapter of your life.

Blessings and Prayers,
Rev. Elaine J. Clinger Sturtz

CHAPTER 2

GRIEF IS A JOURNEY

You have experienced the loss of a loved one, and you are now beginning this journey called grief. This journey is as unique and individual as you are. Common characteristics of grief are *sadness, pain* and *life changes*, but your grief is your own.

You will find this pathway is not neat and organized, nor does it follow a plan or stages. It is all over the place and looks more like scribbles on paper than organized steps. That is okay. Our lives are not neat and organized all the time; therefore, grief becomes a part of the chaos of our lives.

Grief has no right or wrong way. Grief can be very intense for a period of time, and after a while the intensity comes and goes depending on events, triggers or just life. You are still on the pathway of loss, but there are moments of calmness.

Our mourning has no time frame. We will always grieve the loss of our loved one but in different ways throughout our lives. As time passes, we are able to remember and talk about our loved one without the intense pain and emotional turmoil. Those intense times will come but will not last as long. We learn to live with the sorrow and mingle it with the love of a life lived.

Give yourself permission and time to grieve. You may be a more private person and need to grieve alone. You may need the support of family and friends and want to grieve alongside others. If you need support, you may need to ask for it. It is not that others do not care. It is that they are not reminded each moment of your loss as you are. Your life and world has completely changed. While others may have been affected by the loss, their lives have not been turned upside down by it.

As you begin this journey, you may feel you are just existing. You may pretend for the sake of other family members or your job that you are doing well, but inside you only experience turmoil, uncertainty and numbness. You may feel empty inside and disconnected to people and daily life for a time. You are going through the motions of living, but in reality, you are just existing. You are on the path of grief.

You may have a very flat affect—nothing excites you or brings a smile. You are melancholy. You feel very little emotion except sadness. You know there is good and joy around you, but do not believe you will ever experience it again. You see beauty, but it does not move you to feel anything within you.

It is okay. Grief is a process. You have experienced great loss. Your heart is broken. You have no idea how to live and find a new life without your loved one. You don't have to know—you just need to keep walking down this path of grief. Rely on the foundation you had before your loss—your faith, love, and support around you to give you firm footing on the rocky and rugged path of grief.

A hole is in your heart—a hole created from your loved one being ripped from your life. The grieving process does not take away the hole; you just learn to live with the hole. It is the price of love. The caution in the grieving process is not to find a quick fix and fill your heart with unhealthy things or anything just so you do not feel the pain. The important thing is to remember you are on a journey that takes time. No quick resolutions or easy roads are on this journey. All the roads are necessary to take up life again.

Life is different. Life will always be different. This journey is to figure out how to live in the different.

CHAPTER 3

MY GRIEF STORY

Where do I begin? Grief is a part of life. From our earliest memories, we have experienced some type of loss because even birth is a loss—the loss of the safety and warmth of our mother's womb. We experience many types of loss—the death of a pet, the loss of a friend, the loss of the innocence of childhood, the death of a family member. We hear of death somewhere else in the world; we may even say a prayer, but we do not recognize it as a grief to experience.

Then death occurs in my circle of love—the death of a grandparent, a beloved uncle, parents, a grandson and a husband. Grief now becomes personal, and it is my journey to walk and figure out.

As a minister, I have officiated at funerals and walked the journey of grief with many families. As a hospice chaplain for six years, I experienced hundreds of deaths. With some I had developed a long relationship, and others I never had the privilege of meeting. Death is a natural part of life. We try to compartmentalize it and wrap it up in ritual, but death hurts and leaves a wound that cannot be fully healed.

As I began to write this Grief Book, I was trying not to share personal experiences but just my understanding of grief from a clinical and spiritual aspect. Then I realized I was trying to put grief in a neat box of mental health. Nothing is neat and organized about grief. It leaves heartache, pain and a wonder—am I ever going to feel better and be able to function in life again?

I have written about the loss of my Grandma Clinger in my book *Love Lighted Path* and how her love and legacy of faith made a difference in my life. Her life continues to have meaning and purpose through the faith, values and love she shared with her grandchildren. It is passed from one generation to the next. I shared about the death of my grandson, "J.C." in *Glimpses of God* and how the faith of his five-year-old brother, Christopher, made a difference in his grandpa. His childlike faith and belief that his brother was in heaven gave us hope in the midst of our grief. In *The Final Dance of Life,* I shared the fifteen-month journey of caring for Pastor Judy Shook through the disease of ALS and how the Church became the body of Christ and loved her into heaven.

Through the death of my mom, God gave me so many gifts from her life—gifts that I continue to unwrap in my life. I began my running career as a way to deal with her dying and found an intimacy with God in running and praying. Through her gift, I pursued my counseling degree. I miss my mom every day and miss our phone conversations. I miss asking her for guidance and direction. I have come to an acceptance of my parents' death and have discovered how they continue to bear fruit within my life.

I experienced the death of one of my dearest friends. Through this death, I had anxiety I had never felt before and was unable to eat for many days. The loss of someone so dear to me and the heartbreak at the end was devastating. With the support of my husband, I began to walk through the loss instead of denying it.

I share some of the major death and grief experiences to show you a foundation from where I write and began my current grief journey. As a pastor and counselor, I have walked the journey with many people and have counseled them through the loss and the finding of life again.

Nothing prepares you though for the loss of the person to whom you have committed your heart and promised to share life together. The death of my husband changed me forever. I lost the person with whom I shared daily life and shared the joys and frustrations of life. I lost my best friend, my companion, my buddy, the love of my life, my main support and my encourager. The role of a spouse is different in each relationship, but usually a spouse takes on many roles. So, when a spouse dies many gaps are in the surviving spouse's life.

We each have details. What led to the death, the disease, the illness, the accident, the trauma? For some it was tragic and sudden, and for others it was a long, slow, painful decline. For my husband, it was being diagnosed in February with brain tumors, going on Hospice in August, and dying in September.

In my grief, I had time to prepare but never enough time. I thought we talked through all the major concerns and shared the depth of our hearts, but now as most of us, I wish I had asked more and written more down. I wish I had been more attentive, more present, more.... That is when I stopped myself and accepted that at the time, we made the decisions we thought were right. I cannot change the past; I can only live in the present and allow my husband's love to be in my heart forever.

Throughout my husband's illness, death and my journey in grief, I continued to run. I ran with the purpose to release my emotions and cry, not for exercise. Running was my main time to cry through the pain and hurt, and to cry out to God. I remember one day when my husband was changing so rapidly and declining, I cried out to God to release him from this world. I did not want him to die, but it was difficult watching a vibrant, strong, loving husband decline. He had lost the ability to read, focus, walk and be the Dave I knew and loved.

During my husband's illness and after his death, I continued my counseling ministry. It helped me to focus on other people's lives and be able to step out of my own sadness and loss for a while. After his death, God brought to my counseling ministry many more who were also grieving. Because of my own grief, we connected on a deeper level, and I was used by God to walk with them on their grief journey. They ministered to me and helped me to sort through, name and journey further down the path of my own grief.

> "God is the Father who is full of mercy and all comfort. He comforts us every time we have trouble, so when others have trouble, we can comfort them with the same comfort God give us." (2 Corinthians 1:3-4, NCV)

Comfort is to show compassion for another. Compassion is to feel the hurt down inside. It is that "gut-punch" emotion deep within. I had compassion because I had felt the hurt, pain and loss of one so dear to me.

God brought me comfort through others who were grieving and then helped me to bring them comfort out of my own experience. I found and continue to find purpose and meaning in my own loss and grief.

Chapter 4

The Last Day Memories

Our initial memories after death are from the last days of our loved one's life. If death was a slow decline, possibly under hospice care, we watched the physical changes and observed the stages of the dying process. If the death was sudden or unexpected, we wonder if our loved one suffered or experienced pain. We wonder if they knew death was imminent, and did they experience fear or panic? We remember where we were when we received the news of the death. We may avoid the place or have flashbacks each time we encounter the place of bad news.

I remember the shock and numbness when my husband and I received the call notifying us of the death of our eleven-month-old grandson, J.C. My husband, Dave and I were on vacation in Florida and had spent the whole day at the beach. We returned to our rental condo in the evening. A message was left for us to call Dave's son. I can still see the devastation on Dave's face and see him fall into the bed when he heard the voice of his son say, "J.C. died. He choked on a toy at the babysitter's today." Dave screamed and cried and promised his son he would be home as quickly as possible. When we called the airlines, there were no flights until early morning. We spent a few restless and sleepless hours in tears and shock. As we packed, Dave's back went out from all the grief and stress. We left in the middle of the night and waited at the airport for our flight home.

I can still close my eyes and see the room and the deep pain and brokenness on the face of my husband. In a moment, the beauty of the day was gone and death had crashed into our lives. We would never be the same. Death had come too soon and without warning.

When death is gradual, the dying process can take weeks or months or happen quickly over a few hours. It is not about the time frame but the process of letting go of this world. The medical world will share about how the body dies, but there is also a spiritual aspect of the dying process.

In the spiritual process of dying, the body lets go of all that is physical. Therefore, the body uses up all the nutrition within it—this is the reason a person does not eat or drink in the last days and hours. The person uses up all God has put within him/her before letting go of this world.

Everything pulls toward the center of the body—the heart—because this is the only part of the person that remains. The heart and soul is the essence of a person and what is eternal. The heart is the place associated with love. The soul and spirit is the core of who we are, and the essence of our being that lives forever. In the spiritual process of dying, the body releases back into this world all that is not eternal, all that is not love. It is a process of release.

For me, death is a very holy moment. It is when heaven and earth touch, and heaven opens to receive one of God's children. I have had the privilege as a hospice chaplain and as a pastor of being with families as their loved one died. Those images and holy moments remain in my heart and mind.

As a child, my family attended the visitation and funeral services of many extended family members, church family and people from the community. Death was a natural part of life. I was raised on a farm and witnessed the cycle of life through the land and the animals.

My first experience of being with someone in death was when I was in my first appointment as an Associate Minister. Tami was twenty-three years old and dying of cancer. She was just one year younger than I, and we had developed a friendship. I sat with her family through her dying, not knowing what to say. I came to realize that my presence was most important. Her death had a profound effect on my ministry and my life. I saw and felt the pain of loss, the need for compassion but also the holiness in the moment of death.

My years as a hospice chaplain gave me experiences of witnessing these holy moments and last days. I sat with Doris as she left this world so peacefully as the family shared memories and gave her permission to let go. Doris and I connected from the moment we met. She trusted me and had asked many questions about dying. Because of our connection, God gave me the privilege of being with her as she took her last breath.

I sat with Jo and her family as they celebrated her long life. She told them she was ready to go and was at peace. Her death was so gentle and peaceful. I sat with Norma's family as she was taken off the vent and died. I was with Maude when the facility dog jumped up on her bed, licked her face and she died peacefully. I sat with Fred who was all alone in his room. I sang to him and prayed with him as he opened his eyes and looked up on the wall. He closed his eyes and died a few minutes later. I was in the room with Margaret as her brother sang to her, kissed her and she died. I stood beside Jeffrey's bed along with his pastor and another chaplain as we prayed him into heaven.

I had the privilege of being with many hospice patients as they left this world and had the opportunity to say good-bye. I had forged a relationship in their dying, and they were able to share with me their fears, their questions and their hope and peace.

My siblings and I were all present around the hospital bed as my dad died. We had sung hymns with a family friend, Carl, and prayed together. My dad was restless and anxious in his dying, but he was also anxious in his living. I believe we die similarly to how we lived. About five minutes before death, my dad opened his eyes and they were clear as he looked beyond all of us. I assume he was looking into heaven. He closed his eyes and breathed those intense breaths and finally let go.

When my mom died, I was with my siblings and a majority of my nieces and nephews as she left this world. She had gone through the return of her breast cancer and the treatments, spending the last eight weeks of her life in a nursing home. The day before she died, she finally took pain medicine but not enough to control the letting go. My mom kept most of her feelings inside and never complained about the pain of cancer. Therefore, in her last twenty-four hours, her body had to release everything which was stored inside. This was so painful to watch and hear. Now I realize her physical body had to let go of all the pain and everything stored inside of her. It had to be released into this world so that her soul and spirit could be free. Those sounds remained with me for a long time until I accepted this was her way of releasing the pain and suffering of this world.

My husband, Dave, was on hospice care in our home for about a month. We had made the decision to bring in hospice months earlier. I made the call when we were both ready. Dave wanted to die at home with dignity and peace. The hospice nurse was someone I had worked with at a previous hospice, and Dave knew him from his time as a hospice volunteer. The transition was made easier because of the relationship.

The week before death, Dave rallied and was able to walk outside a short distance and attended our weekly life group. Dave said he felt the best he had in months.

As I reflect on the rally, I believe the body needed to release all the energy stored within, and the rally was the release. When the energy was released, the decline happened rapidly.

Our home was filled with friends and family the last days. They brought food, support, prayers and their final good-byes. Two of Dave's friends, Tom and Rob, were with him on Wednesday. Dave went into a deep coma-like state. I received the call that he was declining rapidly. When I arrived at our home within five minutes, Dave was waking up and talking to his friends about going to heaven.

After everyone left and Dave settled, I sat beside his bed and he shared with me about what happened. Dave said that he saw the beautiful, brilliant colors of heaven. He felt a warmth and peace he had never felt. He was able to walk with ease and felt pulled to return. He asked when he could go back. I knew God was preparing Dave to leave this world. God gave us both a glimpse of what was to come so that we would not be afraid. I did not want Dave to leave, but I did not want him to remain in the pain. He could not live in both worlds, and he was longing for the next world. I prayed with Dave that God would allow him to be released from this world and enter the beauty of heaven. We held hands and cried together.

Thursday he was in his hospital bed all day. The aide gave him a bed bath and changed his clothes. It was the last time he spoke. He began to let go. Dave was a fighter all his life—fighting evil in his law enforcement life. His death was loud and intense just like his life. I believe he fought through all the evil he had seen in his life. He always said he wished he had a brain eraser to erase all the bad stuff he had seen in his life. Therefore, in his death he had to release all that was stored in his mind so he could go into the next life. His death was not calm or peaceful, evil never is. Dave was never quiet in life, so his death was not quiet.

We each have details of these last moments which will remain forever in our hearts. The details we may never verbalize fully or even desire to share them with others because of the trauma or the sacredness of the moments.

Once I was able to understand the connection of how my parents and my husband lived to how they died, I was able to be at peace with these last memories. I still remember, but not with the intensity and hurt that my loved ones struggled with in the end, but with an understanding that how they died was how they needed to release what was inside of them and leave it in this world.

You may remember the machines and equipment in your loved one's room. You may have experienced your loved one being taken off the ventilator and that image has stayed in your mind. You wonder if the right decision was made. I experienced being with several families when their loved one was released from the artificial breathing machine. One death was almost instantly after being taken off the machine. Another took several hours, and the family had hope that their loved one would be healed. There were moments and hours of hope, but then a rapid decline and death released their loved one from this world.

The memory of leaving the hospital or facility or waiting for the funeral home to arrive may stay with you. This is the first reality of death. Knowing you will not be going back into the hospital or facility to visit. It is also an emptiness when our loved one's body is removed from our presence. We remember our good-bye. I remember the sadness and anxiousness of our dog, as the funeral directors took my husband's body out of our condo on the cart. I had to hold her close so that she would not follow him.

If you were not present at death, your first memory of death may be at the hospital, the morgue or the funeral home. The reality of the lifeless body makes an impact on our memory and that visual stays in our minds. You may be able to close your eyes right now and see those images.

Your last day memories may include conflict within the family unit. In those last days, the family may not have agreed on decisions, and dealt with the dying in different ways. You may be remembering the disruptions and the turmoil in the midst of your pain and loss. You may need to accept your family and know you could not change the emotions at the time. Death brings out the worst in some people who do not want to deal with the emotions within them. Death also brings up the past and the unresolved conflicts within the family.

Our memories of the last days affect the grieving process. When we relive those hours, either the suddenness of death or the dying process, we need to come to an understanding and acceptance. Otherwise, we remain stuck in a day which can cause nightmares and depression. Talking through the events and letting go of the "what ifs" may help us to move our thoughts from that last day to the life that was lived in the person whom we loved.

Being present at death is a privilege and a gift we give to our loved one. In hospice, I experienced that the right person, the person who needed to be present seemed to be chosen by the one dying. It always amazed me. These last moments can haunt us if we do not process them and understand them as how the body releases itself from this world.

Not being present at death is also a gift. It is the final gift our loved one has to give—not seeing their last breath so as not to have that memory. Either way it is a gift. It is being able to release the guilt and accept the gift.

In the healing of our grief, we begin to replace these intense and painful memories of dying with memories of how our loved one lived. When we remember death, we also need to remember life. The grieving process is like replacing the photo of dying and death with a visual in our minds of the joy and good of our loved one's life. Remember it is a gradual process.

CHAPTER 5

LONELINESS

In our grief, we can feel alone surrounded by family and friends or in a large crowd. We hear the people around us, but the sadness within us creates a wall around us which isolates and builds on the loneliness. It is as if we desire companionship but push people away at the same time.

Loneliness begins that first night without your loved one. You recognize life is different. The shock and numbness are present so you may not feel the loneliness as an emotion. When you arrive home after the funeral or after all the family has gone back to their homes and lives, you recognize the absence of your loved one.

For me, the loneliness became intense after the funeral. The days after the death of my husband were filled with planning the service, preparations, disposing of medical equipment and family arriving. It involved planning meals or finding people to help with meals, making sure everyone was notified and dealing with family. The late afternoon after the funeral when everyone had gone home and it was just me and my dog, I became aware of that intense "gut punch" of being alone. The tears came. I went back to the cemetery and felt the reality of death and was overwhelmed with loneliness.

If you have lost your companion or spouse, going anywhere without him/her feels as though you are entering foreign territory. Your social life may have been couple oriented, and now you are alone feeling awkward in a couple's world. You feel like an extra wheel and find yourself declining invitations. Even at church sitting in a pew by yourself feels strange and lonely though you are in familiar surroundings with caring and familiar people.

Even at family events, it may be difficult to participate without your loved one. Your spouse may have been the outgoing one and was your buffer with family, helping you to feel comfortable. Maneuvering this uncharted territory seems overwhelming.

As you go alone, remember you have a choice. You do not have to do everything or be involved as you used to be. Choose what you feel to be most comfortable and be aware of the feelings you will encounter being alone. You may want to participate in events with grandchildren, family and friends. You have the desire, but you feel out of place without your loved one beside you.

When you are invited to events, parties or time with family, it is alright to say no, not this time. It is also acceptable to go for a short time—make an appearance and then leave. It is also okay to go and enjoy the moments and to laugh in the midst of grief, escaping the loneliness and sadness for a time. This does not mean you have forgotten your loved one. It just confirms that joy and sadness exist in the same moment, and in the midst of the grief is life.

When you have lost your spouse or companion, the loneliness is felt deeply as you eat alone. Some find it difficult to eat in a restaurant alone and choose take out instead. Others choose friends or family to provide companionship at meals though it is not the same. Taking trips or going on vacation may make the loneliness more intense. You wonder how you can go on without your companion or spouse or loved one. It will be different, and it may take some time before you can take that trip.

If you were still employed when your loved one died, you may find yourself working more hours so as not to be alone. Everyone at work talks about looking forward to the weekend or extra time off, but you dread the weekends because you will be alone.

The loneliness also comes when nobody speaks the name of your loved one. Sometimes people intentionally avoid talking about the one who died for fear it will be too emotional for you or they do not know what to say. Speak their names and share memories. Yes, you may cry, but it will help with the loneliness. You remember your loved one lived. Speaking their name acknowledges life. It also gives others permission to share memories and relax in your presence.

Loneliness comes when you reach for the phone to call your mom or dad and realize your parent is gone. You desire to say "Hi, Daddy." When my dad died, I missed being called "Daddy's little girl." While I still was his little girl, nobody spoke these words. When my Mom died, I missed saying "I love you, Mom." I missed the phone calls. I called my mom to ask about recipes and how to do so many things. She was the person I called for information. She was my "google person." I felt lonely when I would look at the phone and not be able to call them and hear their voices.

Loneliness comes when you walk into your child's empty room. Everything is neat and in its place because it is no longer being used. You sit on the floor and remember, and loneliness washes over you. Your arms are empty. You long to hold your child or grandchild. Your dreams are shattered.

We each need to find a way to cope with our loneliness, but it is a reality of our grief. We will miss our loved one's presence. Keeping busy helps for a while, but the work is also a way to prolong dealing with the emotions of grief. Busyness will make us tired and cause us to slow down, rest and begin to embrace the quiet moments.

For me, when I leave an event, party, church service or whatever it is, I talk with my husband on the drive home. Sometimes I talk with my husband's picture when I arrive home about what happened. I acknowledge his presence in my heart. I share what would have happened if he had been there or what stories he would have shared. I share what made me sad, what made me laugh and what made me miss him. Sometimes I feel lonely as I share and I cry. Other times I feel we are together in love, and it brings me comfort. I usually talk with him after I turn out the light at night in bed.

As we recognize the loneliness, the evenings seem the most difficult time. You may have shared an evening meal or it was the time you were together after a long day. As darkness begins, loneliness comes in the inability to see in the shades of the night. If it was your spouse who died, you may experience the loneliness of going to bed alone. Grief is very tiring so for some, sleep is a relief and the bed is a place of comfort. For others it is a lonely place. It may be helpful to continue to say good night and recognize your loved one is with you in spirit and love.

Going alone and the feelings of loneliness become a part of the journey. The feelings may remain in your heart forever, but the intensity may come and go. For those with a faith, we recognize we are never alone. God is with us and travels the journey of grief with us. As we accept the loss, we begin to accept that our loved one is with God, God is with us, and therefore, our loved one is with us in spirit. We are never alone.

CHAPTER 6

FEELINGS AND EMOTIONS
OF GRIEF

Grief brings a wide range of emotions. However you feel is okay. Nobody can tell you not to feel a certain way. These are *your* emotions. You are the one who has experienced deep pain and loss. Accept that this is how you feel at the moment and that these feelings and emotions are part of the grieving process.

At the initial death and loss of our loved one, we may feel shock and numbness. We are unable to comprehend the depth of what has just happened. This shock and numbness is experienced as a way of coping through this huge pain and loss. It helps us through all the events surrounding a death—funeral planning, visitation, funeral and burial. We may feel so numb that we just go through the motions of these rituals. Our human mind and body has not had time to feel the hurt and loss so the numbness and shock protect us until we can begin to work through the emotions.

Death may come suddenly, and we feel a deep hurt or "gut punch" within us. The hurt and pain is so intense that everything feels surreal. We are numb and feel like

31

we are living a nightmare, hoping to wake up soon. Some people describe it as a "smack in the face" reality. The shock hurts, and being suddenly hit with the reality of death is overwhelming.

If the death came from a long illness or time of pain and suffering for our loved one, we may feel a sense of relief that our loved one is no longer suffering. Along with the sense of relief, we may feel guilt for being thankful our loved one is no longer suffering because then it seems we are happy about the death. These feelings are real and part of the grief journey for many who grieve.

Our emotions in grief are hard to define. We feel the intensity of the loss and feel mixed up and confused. To reuse a metaphor, it is like being in a snow globe. We feel all shaken with our world twirling around. Then there is a settling for a moment, but someone shakes us up again, and we have no control of our emotions.

Naming the feelings is difficult at first. It is hard to decipher how we feel through the fog of our loss. As we begin to recognize and name our feelings, we can begin to express them and find healthy ways to cope.

Sadness is the most common feeling in grief. The sadness is that our loved one is not physically with us. The sadness is for the loss of our relationship, our future and of the only life we know. One expression of sadness is through crying. Tears are a cleansing of the soul and how we express hurt, pain and loss. Some may cry openly and others privately or within their heart. At first, the tears may be intense and gut-wrenching sobbing.

Tears become difficult to control. Sadness goes with us throughout our grief. We have lost someone whom we have loved. We will be sad. In our sadness, we may find ourselves withdrawing more from people and social situations.

Denial is part of our coping strategy as we begin living in the grief. We may deny our feelings because it hurts too much to feel. We may live in denial by not talking about the death and change in our lives, hoping that it will go away. Others around us may not talk about our loved one anymore because they don't want to deal with the emotions surrounding the death. Denial just complicates our grief and prolongs the process of naturally grieving the loss.

Anger is an emotion we do not like to admit is a part of our grieving process. We may be angry at the circumstances of the death—that more was not done or if it could have been prevented. Sometimes we are angry at the person who died because they left us alone. The anger sometimes is that the wrong person died in the family. A family member may state that it should have been them because they have lived a long life. The unfairness of death is part of the anger. We ask the "why" questions and have no answers. We become angry that death does not make sense.

Anger is a natural emotion that needs to be expressed. If turned inward, anger can become depression and turned outward, anger becomes violence. A healthier way is to talk through your anger. You can yell and scream in the privacy of your home or out in the woods.

Anger is a physical emotion, and therefore, something physical needs to be done to help release this anger that builds inside. Find a healthy way like walking, running, cleaning, sewing, or some labor-intensive activity to release the anger.

Anxiety comes in many forms in grief. Anxiety is the fear of the unknown. We have anxiety also from the regret of the past. "If only I had…." is a common regret in grief. We allow our minds to wonder to the past trying to answer the why questions. "Why did he have to die?" "Why did she leave me now?" "What could I have done to prevent it?" "Why is God punishing me?" When we live in the past, our anxiety of regret and shame take over.

Anxiety is also worry and fear for the future. The fear is of being alone and unable to make decisions. We have no idea what to do next, how to live without the one we love. Our fears take over.

As we experience this heightened anxiety, it may lead to a panic attack. Some basic coping skills are helpful in our grieving process. In a panic attack, the first thing to do is to breathe and focus on slowing down the breathing. Next is to focus on your surroundings and center yourself into the moment. Name what you see, hear, smell and taste. This slows you down and takes your mind off what caused the moment of panic.

The skill of self-talk is a healthy way to deal with anxiety. Self-talk is being able to step back from a situation and talk yourself through it. This may be done quietly within your thoughts or spoken out loud. It slows you down and helps you to be reflective. It is also helpful to give yourself grace—to forgive yourself when you mess up.

We have no power or control over death. The future is not here yet. We have the present, and we have the love of the one we loved still in our hearts. Nobody can take away that love which will sustain us in the moment.

We may also feel lonely and alone with our loved one physically gone. Loneliness accompanies grief. It is helpful to talk with others who have had a similar loss. They have an understanding of the loneliness. But the reality is life has forever changed, and we will always miss the one whom we have loved so deeply and who gave meaning and companionship to our lives. A hole will be in our heart, but that is because we have loved. We are who we are because of that life and love. Allow memories to heal and help. Yes, memories and pictures may bring tears, but that is part of the healing process. They remind us that we shared life and are thankful for that life.

Grief causes our thought process to be cloudy. Sometimes it may feel as though we are in a fog. During these times, it is often difficult to make decisions, set goals or even complete ordinary everyday tasks. You are not going crazy; you are just grieving when you feel this way. Slow down. Be patient with yourself. Wait to make major decisions, and ask for help from someone you trust before you make any needed and immediate decisions.

Our thoughts may take us down paths that are not healthy and keep us awake at night, raising our anxiety. Sometimes in the grief journey, we have to apply the coping skill of thought blocking and stop thoughts that are harmful. This practice is one of recognizing that what is going through your mind is not healthy and saying to yourself, "Stop." Do not go down that path. It is not healthy. For some people it is helpful to visualize a stop sign and literally stop the thought. Another helpful coping technique is to talk through your thoughts, and then let them go. Some people find it helpful to also write out their thoughts in a journal. This is helpful if the thoughts are recurrent.

The emotions of grief go in no order and come without warning. At the beginning of our grief journey, we usually have no control over our feelings and emotions. As we walk the journey of grief, we begin to learn to accept our emotions. Our goal is to find ways to work through the feelings and develop healthy coping skills. We do not want to deny or suppress the emotions because that will complicate our grief and distort how we are really feeling.

Our feelings and emotions affect our behaviors, too. We are more absent-minded and have trouble remembering details and what we need to do. Making a list is helpful when taking care of the details after a death.

Our emotions of grief may change our sleep patterns. We may have trouble falling asleep and wake up throughout the night. We may want to sleep and not get up in the morning, too. Our sleep is disturbed because of our thoughts and our emotional turmoil.

Our appetite may also change in our grief. Some people cannot eat and others seem to eat everything in sight—that is, they eat their emotions. We may crave unhealthy food—sweets and lots of carbs or comfort food. It is trying to find a healthy balance that will help regulate our emotional swings.

One of the behaviors related to the emotions of grief is sighing. I have become aware that in my grief I sigh so much more—especially at moments when I realize my husband is not here, and I cannot share how I am feeling with him. I sigh. Sighing helps to release my grief and that release of air seems to calm my spirit. Try sighing. Sighing is referenced in the Bible. Paul talks about not knowing how to pray. The Holy Spirit intercedes for us "...with sighs too deep for words." (Romans 8:26, RSV) Sighing in our grief is releasing to God what we cannot put in words.

However you feel is okay. Do not allow anyone to tell you how to feel or that you should not still be grieving. No feeling is wrong. You feel this way right now, but you do not have to stay in the feeling. Emotions will come and go during the grief journey. The journey at times may feel like an emotional roller coaster. Allow yourself to ride, and in time, the intensity will slow down, and you can get off the roller coaster.

CHAPTER 7

PASSAGES OF GRIEF

Our lives are a series of passages from one stage of life to the next. We are born, go to school, graduate and leave home, get married, work and retire. Life continues to change. Each passage is like a new chapter in our book of life, and each chapter is different. In a book, each chapter builds on the previous chapters and flows together. In life, we learn from each passage or chapter and take what we have learned and gained into the next passage of life. We are always moving into the next chapter and learning to let go. We learn from those with whom we share that passage of time.

We have encountered a chapter of loss. We have had to let go of someone we have loved deeply. The loss reminds us that life is not perfect and life does not work out as we had planned or expected. In our grief journey, we have a choice on how to deal with our great loss. We can give in to our emotions and live in anger, hurt, hate, resentment and blame. Or we can choose to allow our loss to be another passage or chapter in our lives and search for new hope and new life.

My Grandma Clinger was the most influential person in my life. It was through her faith and her continuous prayer for me that I heard God's call. She lived her faith through her gentle acts of care. I have always followed her example throughout my life, and now in my grief and loss of my husband, I again have my Grandma to follow. She was a widow for thirty-six years and lived life in those years. She moved from the farm to a home in our small town. She stayed active in her church, her mission work, her hobbies and with her family. While she grieved the love of her life, she lived in the midst of her grief and loneliness. Each day she planned something she could look forward doing. She has given me an example to follow in this chapter of my life.

Death and loss is a natural part of the journey of life. The loss of our loved one was not something we expected or desired, but we can choose to see it as a passage. It is a passage of our lives into another form of love.

When our loved one died, it was not the end to that love. Their spirit of love remains within us. First Corinthians 13:8 states, "Love never ends." (RSV) The person we have loved remains in our hearts in a deep and intimate way. Our loved one is a part of our heart, a part of who we are. Because we walked the journey of life together, our loved one has made a difference and influenced who we have become.

As we journey through our grief, we begin to accept that our loved one is never going to be physically present.

We begin to recognize that his/her love is with us in a new way. We give thanks for our loved one's life. We remember how we shared life together and celebrate the memories. We recognize the legacy of his/her love. Our loved ones continue to live on in the love, and the fruit of their lives continues to bear fruit in our lives. Their love begins to transform us into a new life.

The passage from life to death is also a passage to life. It is an eternal love that remains with us and guides us into this next chapter of life. Passages have no time structure or limits, just like grief. Take your time in this chapter; you will know when you are ready to venture into the next chapter.

CHAPTER 8

DEALING WITH POSSESSIONS

As you look around your home or the place your loved one lived, there are possessions they owned that now hold a different meaning. This is the tangible evidence that they lived and are reminders of their lives.

Open the closet, and you see clothes worn by your loved one. On shelves, in drawers or in the garage are possessions that now describe the life of the one you loved.

One of the questions on our grief journey is "What do I do with my loved one's material possessions?" For some of you, the decision needs to be made quickly if your loved one was in a rental place, a facility or the place is being sold.

For children cleaning out the home of parents, it is "What do I keep? Who in the family gets what?" How are those decision made? My Grandma put names on the back of her possessions or wrote a list of who in the family received which item. She made the decisions so her family did not have to decide. My mom wanted her five children to make the decisions together. So, we met

43

and went through her home with each sibling choosing what he/she wanted, and if we all wanted the same item, we drew names. It worked for us, and we all got along.

The complications come when family members disagree and have unhealthy relationships. The fight over possessions can destroy families and complicate the grieving process. It takes away from the legacy of our loved one.

We each have to deal in our own way with our loved one's possessions. You may feel pressure to make quick decisions which you are not ready to do. Wait. Even if you need to move the possessions quickly because they are in a rental place or facility, you can always store them in your current location or a storage unit, giving yourself time to sort through the life collection of your loved one.

If you have the space and are not moving, there is no need to hurry the process as long as you feel comfortable living in the midst of your loved one's possessions. Do not feel required to change your home. You are the one who lives there. Everyone has an opinion; listen to your heart.

To determine your next steps, you need to recognize the type of person you are. Do material possessions have meaning? Are you a collector of things? What do the possessions represent to you? Did you give, donate or discard items before the death of your loved one? Are you an orderly, everything has its place and purpose kind of person? Recognize if you are a saver or a giver. This will help you determine your path.

As I began to write this chapter, my mind drifted back to the three residences my husband, Dave, and I lived in during our marriage. I began to walk in my mind through each room, touch the furniture and look at the wall hangings that were once treasured but now given a new home. The memories still remain and bring joy within my heart.

My husband was a collector of stuff. He enjoyed the Red Barn Flea Market which inspired the collections of ceramic birds, anything brass and a variety of knickknacks. He added to his American Indian collection, and bookstores increased his library collection. When we downsized to a condo during his illness, many of these collections found new homes, but an abundance of them found their way into the condo.

I am not a collector of things, and I gained this understanding when I was thirteen years old and our family home was destroyed by fire two days before Christmas. I learned the valuable lesson that relationships with those you love are more important than any possessions.

When you have space and one person enjoys the treasures, you compromise and celebrate the gifts. When my husband died, I created a memory box of special items and scrapbooked pictures of memories of our life together. Certain items remained close to my memories so they are displayed in my current home. I began to give away Dave's possessions, not because I did not want to remember or it hurt too much to see them. I wanted to give a piece of Dave to others so that they could have a tangible remembrance.

I gave to his children and grandchildren the items that were in the Sturtz Family and were a part of the family before I married Dave. I still find items that remind me of someone in the family and give the gift of the memory and the material possession.

When you look at the clothes in the closet of your loved one, it may be too difficult to part with any of them for a while. That is okay. Choose an item or two that is very special to you. Hang them in a special place or choose to wear them as a way of feeling close to your loved one.

Some people have stuffed bears or pillows made from loved one's clothing and then give them to members of the family to treasure. Some make quilts from their loved one's T-shirts. I have a necktie quilt made from my husband's favorite ties. The quilt now hangs in my bedroom. I touch it daily as a reminder of his loving presence.

Giving away clothing and personal items of your loved one is emotional. It is working through the feeling that you are giving away the person and your relationship. I view it as sharing my husband with others and keeping his legacy alive—his love keeps giving to others.

Another area of "what do I do with?" is the gifts received from the funeral—those who give remembrances.

The flowers take care of themselves, and the plants continue as long as you tend to them. But what do you do with the sentimental stones, the blankets, the wind chimes and all the other beautiful items given in memory of your loved one?

Keep the ones that mean the most to you or are from those who mean the most to you. Share with family and friends so they have physical reminders too. Donating to a nursing facility, a homeless shelter or another organization is also a way to pass on the legacy of your loved one. Do not feel obligated to keep something just because someone gave it at the funeral. It may not be a healthy reminder for you.

Take all the time you need to make decisions on material possessions. Nobody can take away the memories. You decide what physical reminders you need and want to keep. Scrapbooks, pictures and memory boxes are great reminders and evidence that your loved one lived life.

CHAPTER 9

BEREAVEMENT (MEMORY) BOX

As you begin to organize the material possessions your loved one acquired during life, you will encounter special mementos that describe your loved one. These are treasures that you will want to keep as reminders. They give meaning and purpose to your loved one's life and are continuing reminders of how they lived, what they accomplished and how they touched your life and the lives of others.

These mementos may include some of the following: letters, cards, jewelry, photos, medals, awards, favorite things, memorabilia and just little things that remind you of your loved one. It may be a souvenir from a trip, a ticket stub from a game, a bulletin from church, a playbill, something that makes you laugh. Whatever it may be, collect all those things that are reminders.

Then, create a memory box. It may be a box purchased in a store, a shoe box or whatever you may choose. Place all these items in this box, and store your box in a place in your home. Whenever you need to feel close to your loved one or just want to remember, pull out your box and go through the memories. You may cry, laugh and have every range of emotion. That is fine; it is part of the grieving process. You may want to keep the box as only *your* special box, or you may want to share it with family and friends over time and share the memories and stories behind each item in your box.

While I have many items throughout my house that are reminders of my husband, I have two special boxes. One box contains all the letters and cards my husband wrote to me throughout our dating and marriage. These letters are priceless to me. The words describe his love, and his handwriting reminds me that he lived and wrote with his hand what was in his heart. The other box contains a wide variety of my husband's possessions: glasses, wallet, watches, rings, a pen, name tags and ID, pocket knife, keys and so many other little things that remind me of my husband. I randomly open the box, hold the items and remember that these items were touched by him and important to him. They are material reminders that he lived; they are reminders of the uniqueness of his life.

CHAPTER 10

THE LANGUAGE OF GRIEF

When our loved one died, we may have used the words that our loved one "passed" or that we "lost" our loved one or they "went to be with the Lord." We use different terms to describe death to ease the pain of our grief.

The language of understanding is in grief. When we encounter someone who has experienced a loss similar to ours, we may connect with them on an emotional level. We feel they have an understanding of the deep pain and loss we feel. They have the spirit of grief within them.

The level of conversation deepens to an emotional connection when we encounter someone who has experienced a loss similar to our own. We listen with emotion and empathy and share feelings and stories that we may not even share with family and friends. No judgment of our continued grief or any "you shoulds" is expressed, just genuine "I understand" "I've been there" emotion.

Those who have not experienced deep grief and loss do not understand why we continue to grieve. It does not make sense to them that we could still feel pain, hurt and heartache. Living with the wound, while it may look healed on the outside, the heartache and hole in the heart remains.

We may have also experienced the language of the dying. If our loved one went through a decline and process of dying, hopefully we had the opportunity to have some meaningful conversations and speak from our hearts the words of love. These conversations may have included a time of forgiveness and grace, a time of "thank you" and an expression of love and a sharing of what the person meant to you. While these conversations can be difficult, they assist in the grieving journey, knowing you have spoken aloud the words from your heart.

Many people never have this opportunity because of the suddenness of death or inability to speak or comprehend. Then these conversations occur after death in our grieving process. We may talk with our loved one through a picture, an empty chair or at the grave. It is not the same as a personal conversation, but it is a way to have some closure and express what is in our hearts. These conversations become our "good-bye for now" or "see you later" conversations.

In the talking through our grief, our mind processes and comes to an acceptance quicker than our heart. We know in our mind that our loved one is physically gone, but sometimes our hearts feel as though they will walk through the door. Our minds know they are no longer suffering or in pain, but our hearts want them back in our lives. Our faith assures us they are in heaven and with God, but our hearts ache for them to be with us instead.

It is difficult to put into words our grief and explain the roller coaster of emotions. We may look and act like we are handling the loss, but inside there is so much chaos. When someone asks, "How are you doing?" we usually reply, "I'm fine." It is only to those who also grieve that we can say, "I'm struggling," and they accept our emotion, not trying to change us or make us feel guilty for feeling this way. In my grief, my response to how I was doing became "It's tough, but I'm trying." That was the truth. It was the genuine language of my current grief.

It is a risk we take in our grief to actually share how we are feeling. It is being able to find people who understand grief and will listen and just be present with us. Because sometimes when we share, a judgment is placed on us that we are still grieving and have not moved on. Do not listen to these words. Grieve in your own time frame, and when you need help processing through the grief, seek help and guidance.

The language of grief is confusing and mixed with emotions that have no reasoning or order. That is grief, and that is alright.

CHAPTER 11

TALKING THROUGH THE GRIEF

P art of the emptiness that you feel in grief is that you cannot talk to your loved one face to face. You miss the conversation and the ability to communicate either in person or by phone every day. You miss the sound of your loved one's voice, and at times you think you hear that voice if but for an instant. That voice is so familiar that it lives within you, but you fear that it will fade with time.

As you walk through your grief, sometimes it becomes helpful to still talk to your loved one. Things may have been unresolved and never spoken. You may have feelings of anger that you keep buried inside but wish you could say to your loved one. You want to release those emotions.

We heal in our grief if we continue to talk with our loved one. Some people talk to a chair and envision their loved one sitting there listening. Other people talk to a picture of their loved one. Some people go to the cemetery and talk to their loved one's grave. Whatever you choose, it is helpful in your grief to talk to your loved one just as if he/she were alive.

It is helpful to talk out your emotions and to talk about your love, your loneliness, your sadness, your hurt, your thankfulness for your loved one's life and all the other emotions that are within you. As you make decisions for your present and future, you may even want to talk them out with your loved one like you used to. That way you include them in your life and remember how they would have responded.

It is saying "good morning" and remembering and knowing the love goes with you each day. It is sharing your day with your loved one like you used to and knowing your loved one lives within your heart. It is saying "I love you" and remembering the love you shared. It is saying "good night" and thanking God for the gift of having your loved one in your life.

All this conversation guides you in keeping your loved one in your life, just in a different form. The love never ends, and the conversation is part of the love shared. Therefore, the daily conversation doesn't need to end.

Over time the conversation may not be as intense. You may smile as you pass their picture and pause and say "hello." You may see something that reminds you of your loved one in your day and say, "I remember when you ...." This does not mean you have stopped caring; it just means they are within your heart. Your grief has now journeyed to an intimacy that no longer needs to be spoken.

Talking through your grief may also include talking with a counselor, a faith leader or a trusted friend. It is being able to speak aloud your feelings, emotions and struggles to gain a new perspective and also to hear yourself name the grief. It is a healthy process in our grief.

CHAPTER 12

CHANGE IN STATUS

As I filled out the form, I came to the marital status question: single, married, divorced, widowed. For the first time, I realized my status had changed. I could no longer mark "Married" because another choice described my current status: "widowed." Oh, the emotion of the change in three letters from wife to widow.

The change may also be in your emergency contact person and "go to" person. If that person was the loved one who died, your safety and security has become vulnerable. You have to re-establish whom you trust and whom you depend upon.

This change is also noted in how mail is addressed. We are no longer Mrs. John Doe; we are now Ms. Jane Doe. Our husband's name is no longer associated with our name. For a widower, sometimes the status change becomes "you are now available." Well-meaning friends or family try to "fix" you up with somebody. You feel you are being pushed too quickly into a new relationship when you need to grieve the loss of your beloved spouse.

For some of you the change in your status is from having parents to being an orphan. When my mom died, I realized I was an orphan. An orphan is a person without parents. I had become a part of the oldest generation. My status had changed.

In the loss of a sibling, you begin to rephrase how you state the number of siblings. You now state how many are living and how many are in heaven. You do this knowing you will be asked about your siblings' location.

For others at the loss of a child, you have become childless according to society. If it was your only child, your status as a parent has changed.

While these are titles or statuses of how society categorizes people, it leaves out the love relationship that has occurred and that cannot be broken. You will always have parents in your heart. The memories and influences of them upon your life have made you who you are today. Love never ends, and the bond of love in a marriage remains in your heart forever. The love of a child, the part of you that created the child, never dies.

But with the categories, we recognize the change that has occurred in our lives and in our relationships. We are different. We relate differently. We identify ourselves in a new way, and it seems so unreal and unwanted.

The change is not just in titles or forms, but in relationships. If our spouse or companion died, we are no longer part of a couple. Our status and relationship with friends has changed. We may be excluded from social events that are couple-oriented, or if we are invited, our status is no longer a "couple."

If you lost a child, your relationship with other parents has changed. You may no longer be included in events since your child has died. Other parents may not want to make you sad when they share the accomplishments of their children, so you are not included in conversations and relationships.

If you lost your parents, what changes for you is when you hear friends and co-workers complain about their parents or having to do something for them, and you become angry. You wish you could be the caregiver for your parents. You begin to step away from those who are complaining. You are an orphan, and others now assume you don't understand anymore. You long to speak the words, "Dad" and "Mom" again.

The change in status is emotional. We have to define who we are now. This is part of the journey.

CHAPTER 13

LIVING IN THE MIDST
OF THE GRIEF

As we grieve, we feel as though our life is in a holding pattern or that we are going in circles and not going anywhere. We feel we are just existing and wonder if a time will come when we will live and move forward from the grief. The concept of moving forward feels as though we are letting go of the one we love and, therefore, we do not want to move forward without them. Grief is not linear. Grief is the emotional feeling of loss that remains with us, and we learn to live in the midst of our loss which has changed life forever.

Grief does not end, because the love we have never ends. Therefore, we learn to live in the midst of grief and find life. The pain of loss and the grief becomes a part of who we are. We find life in the midst of the suffering and pain, and it teaches us compassion for others. The wounds of our grief heal, but the scar remains as a reminder of the love that lives within us.

As we journey down this road of grief and wrestle with our faith in the midst of the grief, we begin to learn how God uses our suffering, pain and loss to help us grow and move closer to God. Our faith may be tested in our loss, but inviting God into our grief means that we will never walk the journey alone. It is learning to trust God even when we do not understand and there are no answers. It is holding on to a hope of a hope. Hope has to do with who God is, not what our circumstances are.

When we grieve, we recognize that what also died is who we were. Our identity is intertwined with the one who died. When we lose a spouse, we lose our identity as a wife or husband. It is our public image and identity that is lost. Our grief challenges us to face our loss and look inside of ourselves. We come to understand that who we are in the eyes of God has not changed; we are still loved, still a child of God and still have God's loving spirit within us. This is when we begin to live in the midst of our grief and mingle the love and sadness together into a life.

Life is filled with changes from one chapter to the next. There is a sense of grief as we look back and remember each chapter. A small death has occurred in each passage. We leave behind childhood to become an adult. We leave one job for the next. We leave our parents and our childhood home to be married and establish a new home and a new life. With each change comes a new opportunity, and each small death gives us new life.

Each change or chapter is a part of who we are. They build upon one another and lay the groundwork for the next chapter of life. We have to go through each one to become who we are meant to be. We need to learn from each—learn from the good, the challenges and the hurt. Each of the events and people create us into who we are. We learn to love, which can bring pain and sadness, but we are forever changed and made stronger because of the love. We would love all over again even though we know it would bring hurt, pain and grief.

As we remember our loved one and the life we shared together, we bring what we learned, how we grew through the relationship and who we have become in the present. New life is given to these memories because we continue to learn from our loved one's life. Memory is a foundation that anchors us. We learn from the past, and we bring the past into the present life. This foundation opens us up to a hope for the future.

The love we have shared with our loved one continues in our hearts, giving us hope and trust in a future. We are never alone. We will always miss the ones we loved, but their love goes with us forever through all we learned while in relationship with them. We learn to live in the midst of missing them physically and find a life in which their love remains in our hearts.

We experience living when we focus on our loved one's life, not on his/her death. When the focus is on how death occurred and all the issues of the death, it is hard to process, and we remain stuck in the death. When we begin to focus on their life, who they were, how they made a difference and who we are because they lived, then we start living in the midst of our grief.

It is not about our grief becoming easier or life becoming easier without our loved one. It is about accepting that this is the reality of our lives and living in the midst of the grief.

CHAPTER 14

COMPLICATED GRIEF

G rief has many aspects, and it takes time to sort through them and make any sense out of the journey. At times our grief is messy, with many interconnecting parts that become tangled. It becomes tricky to walk through the grief. This is called complicated grief.

Other professionals define complicated grief more as being stuck in your own grief and not being able to accept that your loved one has died. It is being so preoccupied with your loved one that it affects all relationships and your daily living. This is one aspect of complicated grief. I am focusing on issues that prevent the grieving process.

There are many issues that may complicate the grieving process. You may have experienced multiple deaths within a short period of time. Therefore, you have not had time to grieve one loss before another one has occurred.

Our emotions and attitudes may complicate the grief process. If we are unwilling to accept the reality of death and live in denial, the grieving process cannot begin. Acceptance does not mean we are fine and can function in daily living. It just means we are facing the reality that our loved one has died, and we admit our own pain, hurt and loss.

The words that friends and family have said may complicate our grief. They may have meant to comfort or try to explain the death or even answer the "why" questions, but their words have not brought comfort or peace. The statements have made us question our faith, our emotions and even our relationships—statements like: "I know how you feel." "It's for the best." "He's at peace now." "She is in a better place." "It's good he's not suffering anymore." "God doesn't give you any more than you can handle." "It's God's will." "It's a blessing." These are all words *not* to say at a funeral, visitation or at any time there is a death and people are grieving. They are not helpful.

So what words bring comfort? The less spoken the better. Comfort comes in being present, a touch or a hug. I suggest people say, "I'm sorry for your loss." And if you knew their loved one personally, to then share a memory or story. By so doing, you share how their loved one was in relationship with others, made a difference and gives meaning to their loved one's life. It also helps the grieving process.

The loss of your support system may complicate the grieving process. Your loved one may have been your main support with whom you shared your feelings and emotions. Therefore, you have no outlet to share and provide the familiar support. Another loss of support may be the loss of the staff who assisted in the care of your loved one—hospice staff, nursing home staff, caregivers, friends and family who were daily available to assist with care. They have all moved on to care for others. You may have developed relationships with other families in a facility while caring for your loved one, and now that bond has been broken in death.

Those of you who were the main caregivers have the loss of your role as caregiver. You have lost your routine, the people with whom you have interacted daily, and maybe even your meaning and purpose for your life. You gave everything to care for your loved one, and now you feel empty and alone.

When I cared for Pastor Judy Shook through her battle with ALS, I was daily involved with those who were assisting in her care and with the facility staff. After her death, I had a gathering of the people from the church that assisted in her care. It was a time of closure and gratitude, but it was a time of loneliness for me. We would never again be together with this purpose. As we each went back to our families and routine, the sadness and loss of these interactions made me grieve in a variety of ways. I first had to grieve the loss of the daily routine I had established with Judy, the daily conversations on her care, and my purpose before ever beginning to grieve the loss of my colleague and friend.

Another issue that complicates our personal grief is our role in the family. We may assume it is our responsibility to help others through their grief and be of support to everybody else in the family while delaying our own grief. As parents, you will sacrifice for your children and try to be strong for them while falling apart inside. We may try to make it better for others while denying our own grief.

Relationships with family and friends change when there is a death. Your loved one may have been the foundation of the family, and now it feels as though the family is falling apart. The person who died may have been the one who kept the blended family together. You feel the need to fix it and take on the role of keeping the family together. This is not always your task. Your task is to grieve the loss of your loved one. The unhealthy relationships in a family may prevent grief from running its natural course.

Addiction will complicate grief—whether your own or someone's in your family. Some people will use alcohol, drugs or other addictions as a way to cope with grief. These other additions may include eating, shopping, hoarding, gambling, risk taking and many other unhealthy behaviors. It just complicates grief and helps avoid dealing with the emotions of grief.

When a death occurs, some family members may distance themselves from the family because their main connection was with the one who died. Allow each person to set his/her own boundaries and own way of dealing with the death. You can complicate your grief when you try to keep things the same and take on the role of fixer.

Grief is complicated on its own. The people and events of our lives will make grief messy and confusing. Find your own path on the journey of grief and go down the path.

LeAnne Gompf

CHAPTER 15

UNRESOLVED RELATIONSHIPS

The relationship you had with your loved one may have ended with some unresolved issues or in difficult circumstances. You may have regret from the past, or while you loved them, the relationship may have been unhealthy or filled with turmoil. You never had the opportunity to mend the brokenness of the relationship.

So now in your grief, your heart is broken along with the inability to bring healing to the past. You may be struggling with the death of your loved one due to addiction or bad life choices. You may have been separated at the time of death due to distance in miles or estrangement in relationship.

Now you are trying to navigate this path of grief and have no idea where to begin. One of the ways may include resolving the relationship within your own heart. This may take time as you work through the reasons the relationship was so chaotic. If addictions were involved, the process begins with being able to remember your loved one before the addiction took control. Separating the person from the addiction and focusing on the memories from before the addiction was the center.

Many people find it helpful to write a letter to their loved one expressing the hurt and anger along with all the unanswered questions. Others find it helpful to talk to their loved one's picture or an empty chair and visualize their loved one in the chair.

Whatever you find helpful, the goal is to work through the relationship and let go of the pain and hurt of the past so that you can begin to grieve the life of your loved one. You want to remember the good of their life and the love you have for them and not focus on the brokenness and hurt.

You may choose to seek a professional counselor to assist in this process of resolving the relationship. You cannot change the past, but you can heal from the past and not take the hurt into the present and future. You have enough heartache in the loss.

Remind yourself that your loved one lived. Life wasn't perfect or even good at times. Mistakes were made. Begin to peel away the layers of hurt, conflict and chaos just as you peel the layers of an onion. Name the layers, and release them. Get to the core, name it and forgive. Forgive yourself and your loved one. To grieve, you may need to give and receive grace. You may never be able to resolve the relationship and the complications that went with it. Sometimes you just need to forgive, give grace and let go, so you can grieve the loss of the person and begin to heal.

The conflict that occurs after death within some families complicates the grieving process. Some families disagree on the decisions following a death. Conflict occurs in making funeral arrangements and who is involved in the service. This conflict continues with possessions and dividing property. Emotions are heightened through death. The reality is not all families get along. The conflicts that were present before the death of a loved one become more intense during death and grief. The hurts, conflicts and disagreements of the past influence the turmoil of death. Death sometimes places a larger separation within a family. Forgiveness and letting go needs to become a vital part of the grieving process. You cannot change people but you can change how you deal with them and how much you let them control your life. Setting healthy boundaries becomes a way to accept the relationships and not allow other people's emotions to bring inner turmoil into your journey. You recognize the conflict and accept you cannot fix it.

CHAPTER 16

LIVING IN THE HURT

E ach day goes by, and you exist. You function and do the tasks required some days, and other days just getting out of bed seems far too difficult. Your thoughts take over wanting to change the outcome of your loss. You dwell on what you could have done differently that day—the day your loved one was taken from you. Your thoughts dwell in irrational and distorted ideas. The thoughts seem real to you. You believe if you had done something different that day, your loved one would be alive. Sometimes in that stage between sleep and awake, you try to figure out what change you could make and this nightmare would be over.

You awake and for just a moment all is good. Then you remember, and you fall apart and feel the deep hurt and loss. Living in the reality of loss becomes too hard. You find it easier to live in the "what ifs," but you become stuck in a fantasy that will never be reality.

As you slowly begin to face today, this is the truth. Your heart aches, and you feel the deep hurt of your loss. You don't like your reality, but this is the life you have.

How do you live in this hurt? Nobody and nothing in this world can make the hurt and heartache better.

This is life now. It is finding a purpose in the life lived—not in the death, but in the life lived, no matter how many days and years that life was here on earth. We can choose to dwell in the hurt and stay stuck on the merry-go-round of existence. It is not pleasant, and going around and around eventually makes you physically sick.

As for me, I began to recognize God walking with me in the hurt and pain. God did not take away the loss and pain, but He walked with me through it. We have this assurance from Psalm 23:4 – "Even if I walk through a very dark valley, I will not be afraid, because you are with me...." (NCV) God does *not* punish us for our sins by taking away our loved one. Life just does not make sense. There are no answers to the "whys" of life. We learn to live in the questions.

When I experienced the death of our eleven-month-old grandson, J.C., I had no answers to why he died. In my book, *Glimpses of God*, I shared about his baptism as I held him in my arms and dedicated him to God. Within eight months, he was gone and was in the arms of Jesus in heaven. The pain and loss was intense for my "official" grandson. J.C. was the grandson born after I married into the family.

I recognized the intensity of the weeping for a child. Jeremiah 31:15 describes this crying: "A voice was heard in Ramah of painful crying and deep sadness: Rachel crying for her children. She refused to be comforted, because her children are dead." (NCV) The death of a child creates a deep and painful sadness. Nothing brings comfort. It is learning to live in the hurt and knowing life will always be different.

Nothing could change the death of my grandson. The only thing that could change was how I reacted to it, and what I did to give his life purpose and meaning. Through baptism, I found a way. I changed the way I officiated at baptisms. Each time I baptize a child, I remember holding J.C. and the precious gift a child is to a family. After the vows and the actual baptism, I walk with the child throughout the congregation introducing the child to the church family. I want the church family to see the child whom they have agreed to support and help guide to love Jesus. Through J.C., I see the importance of this relationship and connection. I share that the child has come from God and someday will go back to God. The church family's purpose is to help guide the child to knowing and loving Jesus.

When I think of J.C. now, I picture him in heaven. He is happy and with his Grandma and now his Grandpa, Dave. I believe he welcomed his Grandpa into heaven. This is where I find hope and healing.

"And this hope will never disappoint us, because God has poured out his love to fill our hearts. He gave us his love through the Holy Spirit, whom God has given to us." (Romans 5:5, NCV)

Many parents, who have lost a child, find a cause to put their love and energy into to continue the life of their child. The parents mourn the loss of the future of their child. The future is lived out in a different way through a cause or purpose. I will let Mike and Sue Murphy tell their story:

> Becoming parents was such a joy for us. Jason was born ten weeks early. After watching him grow and develop for sixty-seven days at Children's Hospital in Columbus, we were delighted to bring him home and start our life as a family. Nineteen years of memories, that's what we treasure. We could never have guessed when we brought him home from Children's Hospital that we would only have such a short time with him.

> We still remember the phone call as if it was yesterday. The police officer told us we needed to go immediately to the hospital because Jason had been in a car accident. For three days, we sat at Jason's bedside. We then heard the words no parent ever wants to hear—he will not survive.

> Jason had registered as an organ donor when he got his driver's license. A very caring representative from Lifeline of Ohio talked with us. Now our son would become an organ, eye and tissue donor. We were on board because we knew that Jason was a caring young man, and he would want to help someone else. We didn't realize what a gift this would become for us.

> The staff at Lifeline was very supportive in the coming months. We were able to meet Jason's heart recipient, Russ. What an unbelievable experience to hear our son's heart beating in another man. Of

course it made us sad, but knowing Jason's selfless decision had given this man new life pleased us.

Once Jason passed, we had a decision to make. Do we draw our curtains and close ourselves off from everything, or do we find a way to live with our grief? We chose the latter. Because Lifeline had been such a large part in our grieving process, we chose to become involved as Lifeline Ambassadors. We have spent many hours talking to high school classes, staffing health fairs, speaking at different religious services and visiting new transplant patients at the hospital to share the power of organ donation. Has it been easy to tell our story over and over again? No... but yes. We have been involved in the life of Russ and his family. Jason was an only child, and now we have an extended family, a heart family. To share Jason and Russ's story gives us such joy. The involvement with Lifeline has allowed us to continue to live through the hurt.

We have found that faith, family and friends have been so important to us in this journey. With the assistance of friends, we sponsor a Memorial Golf Outing each year. The proceeds are used to fund a graduating senior scholarship at Jason's high school. For us, we have chosen to find a way to take our grief and allow others to share it with us, strengthening us to live in the hurt.

Jason died at age nineteen in an accident. His parents, Mike and Sue, were able to donate Jason's organs and saved the lives of others. They were able to meet and develop a relationship with the gentleman who received their son's heart. Because of this selfless donation, Mike and Sue have made Donate for Life their cause and mission to keep the memory of Jason alive.

The death of a child, no matter the age, makes no sense in our rational thoughts. You cannot figure it out or find a purpose in the loss of an innocent child. Nothing makes sense—the accident, the tragedy, the illness. We will never find a reason or explanation that will satisfy.

The hurt and pain will always remain in the heart of parents and grandparents. You will always long for your child to be in your life. Through the journey of grief, parents learn to live with this hurt and pain, and find a way to carry on the future of their child in their hearts and lives in whatever way possible.

CHAPTER 17

FACES OF GRIEF

I looked into the mirror and hardly recognized the person looking back at me. Who was I? I didn't remember. I was numb and just going through the motions of life. I was able to get up, walk my dog and go to work, but coming home at night to an empty house left me broken. This was my first face of grief.

At first, grief leaves us not even recognizing who we are and the life around us. We function and at times appear to even do well according to the outside world. Grief has a mask. We put on the face and go through our day, but it is when we are alone and the mask comes off that we fall apart and wonder if life will ever get better. We think we have to be strong and wear the mask to make it easier for those around us. It does not really help the grief, but it does protect us from the worry and words of others. This is another face of grief—our mask.

We cry and cry and cry and then cry some more. Some of the tears are visible but most are within our soul. We cannot describe how we feel, nor do we know what to do with the emotions if we could name them. Nothing seems to change this raw emotion. We may try to hide it from others. Sometimes we find a compassionate soul that allows us to cry and doesn't tell us to stop nor try to console us with empty phrases. This is our sad face.

We begin to feel guilty that we are making everyone around us sad and feeling sorry for us. This becomes another burden upon us, so we begin to pretend we are doing well. We even go out with family or friends and try to interact and participate even though our heart is not in it. This is our pretend face.

Then we decide to begin to share how we are feeling with those who ask. We try to be honest and share the loneliness, the pain, the hurt and sorrow that are racing through our hearts and minds. We share about our sleepless nights, our fears and our dreams about our loved one. Then we see it—they have no clue. We shared too much and have left our heart open and vulnerable. We try to close the door of our heart and feelings quickly. We race back to our aloneness and look in the mirror and see the "nobody understands my grief" face.

For a while we think we are going crazy. Something must be wrong with us. We ask ourselves, "Why am I still feeling as though I am on a merry-go-round? I keep doing the same thing, feeling the same way and thinking the same things. I thought I was working through my grief, and then bam! Something triggered an intense gut punch, and I am back to where I was." This is the face of "I'm back here again" grief.

Yes, the face of "I'm back here again" comes throughout the journey, but when we look more closely in the mirror, we recognize the place but notice we feel and look different this time. When I began returning to the same place, I began to understand that I would not stay as long this time and that I was changing within and beginning to recognize feelings and emotions. I knew I would walk through this place and remember, but not linger as long. I was just passing through this time. I assumed I would be back again but only to reflect and remember.

This "merry-go-round" ride seems to stay for quite some time. It looks the same and feels the same, but in essence it is not the same. It is almost like the scene in the movie, "Mary Poppins" when they are riding the merry-go-round and the horses are free and ride off the go-round and out into the field. Grief is like this. We may still be on the same horse—the same journey of grief—but it takes on new meaning as we explore. We begin to figure out who we are in this new chapter of our life. We celebrate the life lived and the difference our loved one made in our life. We recognize that we are grateful for the experience of loving, and we accept that we will always love and our hearts will always ache for our loved one. This is who we are. This is the face of love in our grief.

You look in the mirror, and you notice that you are different. Different is not bad, it is just different. You feel like you have made progress through your grief. When the grief becomes intense, you do not plummet endlessly downward. You just fall down and allow yourself to go through the moment, then you pick yourself up. You have begun to talk through the intensity. You pray.

Wow! You realize that you are able to pray again in words, not just in sighs. This is the face of progress you see.

Then one day you look in the mirror. The sadness is not as intense. You notice a little bit of life and light in your eyes. You begin to recognize feelings and emotions and name them. You have a hope that there is life, and that you can live and not just exist. But as you look, you see another face—"who am I now" face appears.

Grief has many more faces. These faces help to define the journey within us. We recognize ourselves in each of the faces and accept that it is okay to be that face. We are a combination of all of the faces at times. The journey of loss helps us to embrace who we are, look within ourselves, and believe in who we were, are and will be.

CHAPTER 18

THE COURAGE TO GRIEVE

Courage, according to Dictionary.com, is "the quality of mind or spirit that enables a person to face difficulty, danger, pain, etc., without fear; bravery." The Apostle Paul ends his letter to the Corinthians, saying, "Be watchful, stand firm in your faith, be courageous, be strong." (1 Corinthians 16:13, RSV)

As you read these words about courage, you may wonder how courage and grief go together. You may feel far from courageous and certainly not brave as the fears and uncertainties of the future surround you. Courage comes from deep within us. Courage is a part of the grief journey.

Courage is being scared and afraid but still going on. That is what you have been doing on your journey. You have no idea what the next step will bring or how you will make it through the next moment without your loved one, but you take the step. That is courage.

Courage is confronting your sorrow. It is giving yourself permission to grieve, to feel sad, to experience a variety of emotions, and to live in the midst of it all.

Courage is saying, "I'm going to go through this. I'm going to express my feelings and not hide my emotions." It is the courage to share feelings honestly and openly. It is taking the risk of being rejected, ignored or shunned by those who do not want to face the devastation of grief.

It is courage when you reach out for help. It takes courage to admit you need help, guidance, support, a hug or just someone with you as you cry. It takes courage to let someone into your grief and see your hurt and pain.

It takes courage to dare to hope in the midst of the pain and hurt. It takes courage to say, "I don't feel hopeful right now, but I believe someday I will have hope and find life again." Courage can be for the future.

Courage is being able to talk with someone who is more recent on the journey than you and to share comfort and your presence. Your heart hears their heart, and you have the courage to stay in the pain and sorrow so as to bring comfort to another hurting soul.

Courage is a God given gift. It is not something that we decide one day that we are going to acquire. Courage comes from deep within our heart. It is part of our faith. Courage sees the fear and is scared, but courage knows it is not alone. Courage and faith walk hand in hand.

CHAPTER 19

LIVING IN TWO WORLDS

Whet is real? Where is my focus? If I make changes, does that mean I forget the past? These and many more questions race through our minds as we walk in our grief. We navigate in our grief through two different worlds. The world of our memories is where our loved one was present and where we found joy and lived life. And now the world of today and tomorrow is a world without our loved one. Our grief is what connects these two worlds.

The world of our past, our loved one and the life we had together holds our thoughts and emotions. We want to stay in the memories and just stop time. We would prefer to go back in time and erase this bad dream, but somehow, we know that is not possible. The alternative is to just stop time and live in the memories. We do this at the beginning of our grieving. Life seems to stop for us while other people go on with their lives. We seem to just mark time with no movement in our lives. The past is our focus, and we live in the memories through pictures, possessions and stories.

We know that life goes on so we try to focus on the moment. Those around you may see that you are beginning to live and heal, and you tell them you are doing well. Your outward appearance looks good, but inwardly, the grief continues to rip at your heart. You are living in two worlds.

You do well for a season, and you think you are moving forward. Then something pulls you under—an anniversary, a picture, a smell—and you go back in your mind to the past while trying to stay in the moment. You are living in two worlds.

You have a desire to jump into life, live in this new chapter of life and accept that your loved one is gone. But the world of the past and your loved one and the life you had holds you back. This is where grief takes work and takes on the task of mingling the past and present together. This is the process of learning from the memories and the fruit of the life of your loved one and bringing them into your current life.

We begin to recognize the gifts of life given to us by our loved one and the strengths gained from our loved one that give us the foundation to begin a new chapter of life. We begin to see the past as a chapter of our life, not a separate world. It is a chapter that has many memories. It is a chapter that we wish had not ended. The memories of this chapter of life are added to our current world. We blend them together to create a new chapter. It is a life that lives in the present but remembers the past as the foundation for our present.

CHAPTER 20

DEFINING YOU

Sometimes it is hard to remember who you were and what life was like before grief, before life became so different. Oh, we go back in our minds to how life used to be and try to remember all the good and allow the bad to fade. We remember events and life shared in relationship, but it is difficult to remember who we were because the current grief clouds our thoughts and heart. We try to remember ourselves laughing and filled with joy. We see glimpses of who we were, but the sadness seems to squeeze out the joy.

We do not return to the place we have already been. We cannot go back to the way life was or the way we were inside. Life is forever different. Are we willing to live in the different? Life is good because I believe God is with us, and God is good. We have changed, so we cannot go back to a normal. This is now our reality. Grief has no end mark. It continues and evolves into different forms and experiences.

What is the same is the love that is within our hearts. Love transcends death. We do not stop loving someone just because they are not physically present with us. The love we have experienced when the person was alive is still in our hearts and is still a vital part of who we are. Love defines us. "But if we love each other, God lives in us and his love is made perfect in us." (1 John 4:12, NCV) When we share love with others, that love is connected with God and never leaves us.

In our grief, we try hard not to feel this love because that is what makes us hurt. Remember the love you shared with your loved one and know you can love them in their absence. When we love in their physical absence, we experience an eternal intimacy that leads to peace within our hearts. Grief is the price of love. When we have loved deeply, we will also grieve deeply.

Because my husband is no longer physically present, I have reflected on the difference he made in my life. He helped define me and influenced my growth, my views and the meaning and purpose of my life. If he were still here, I might not be as reflective and understand the impact made on my life. I begin to define myself from all the memories and bring them into the present, giving my life meaning.

We reflect on who we were with our loved one and the role our loved one had in our life. We recognize the holes left because our loved one is gone. These are the areas we begin to work on so we can be connected to life again.

As we define ourselves, we may take time to re-evaluate our priorities, our goals and how we want to live out our lives. We may make some changes in style, in what we do and where we go. We are different, so we may want to try different experiences. We may reflect and decide we like who we have been and what we have done and want to continue in this same path. Just make sure you are doing it for you, not just because you have always done and think you have to continue doing it for the sake of your loved one. Ask yourself, "Does this bring joy to my soul? Am I passionate about this or do I dread it?"

In defining who you are now, be honest with yourself. Change does not take anything away from your life shared with your loved one. It will enhance your life.

CHAPTER 21

HOPE OF A HOPE

Hope is looking forward to something you expect to happen. It is a belief, a trust in something good. Romans 8:25 talks about this hope: "But if we hope for what we do not see, we wait for it with patience." (RSV)

The idea of hope seems impossible in the midst of grief when life seems so hopeless. Maybe with the death of your loved one, dreams have been shattered and your plans for the future have been destroyed. The future seems so bleak and cloudy with no understanding of how you will survive without your loved one.

You know life goes on. You have witnessed others begin a new life after a loss. They have survived, but right now it may feel like you will not survive this broken heart. It may be possible for others, but it feels so impossible for you right now.

On this journey of grief, sometimes the only hope we can grasp onto is a hope of a hope. It is a belief that just maybe someday you will be able to live and not just exist. You will see beauty in the world, not just a dullness, and you will feel something besides sadness.

I came to understand this hope of a hope through Verna. I met Verna when I was a chaplain for Hospice. Verna was in her 90's with limited mobility and sight. She loved the sunshine and loved to sing the old hymns of her faith. Verna had very little family and needed assistance with almost every daily task and personal care. According to society, Verna was helpless and hopeless. But Verna had a hope of a hope. Someday she would walk and see her Lord in heaven, she would tell me. Verna taught me to have hope in the darkness. I spent weekly visits sitting in the sunshine and singing every hymn I knew from the hymnal. These simple acts brought hope. Verna was not alone in these moments as she felt the warmth of God's love through the sun, and her heart warmed to God's love by singing words of praise.

As I began my own journey of grief, the image of Verna sitting in the sunshine and singing in the midst of a life that was helpless and vulnerable gave me the hope of a hope. I could hope that someday I would have hope and be able to feel the warmth of the sun and sing again. Someday I could live in the midst of my grief. Someday I could find meaning and purpose in my loss and receive peace and comfort. Someday.

You do not need to have hope right now, just hope of a hope.

CHAPTER 22

HEAVEN

We live in a physical world; one that we can see, touch, feel, taste and hear. When we experience the death of a loved one, that physical presence is gone, and that is what we grieve. As we walk this journey of grief and accept the fact they are gone from this world, we may begin to wonder where they are.

Yes, their loving spirit remains in our hearts and the fruit of their labor continues in the relationships of their lives. Is that all? The answer to this question depends upon your faith and belief in a life after this life. For those of us who believe, we would say that our loved one is in heaven with God, our Father and Creator.

This requires a leap of faith to believe in heaven—to believe that when our physical bodies die, there is a place our soul goes and has an eternal heavenly body that lasts forever. It is a place where we are reunited with the saints—all those who have come before us. Heaven is described in the Bible as being present with God and all the believers.

Whether or not you believe in heaven, I would like to share with you my personal experiences of the connection of this world with the spiritual world and heaven.

When I was caring for Pastor Judy Shook, she shared with me her experience of an angel or ministering spirit. On the morning of her 62nd birthday, she awoke and at the foot of her bed, she saw a little boy whom she described as young, blonde and with a smile. She recognized him as an angel, and then he was gone. He gave her such peace and assurance that God was with her on this journey of her disease.

A place beyond this world was confirmed to me through several experiences I had as a hospice chaplain. One experience was sitting with a nurse at the bedside of an elderly sweet lady. She had no family with her, and the hospice staff had become her family. The nurse and I sat on each side of her, and as she died, we held her hands. At the moment she took her last breath, we heard the brush of angel wings ascend with her spirit. We both looked at each other and said nothing. It was such a sacred and holy moment. Only later that day did we confirm with one another what we heard in that room.

Another hospice patient, Don was in a car accident, and because of the accident was in a coma for ten days. While in the coma, Don had a dream that an angel, who appeared as an Indian spiritual man, sat with him. The angel was wearing a tunic that had leggings made of leather, and the cloth had red thread woven in it. He sat beside Don's bed. In this dream, the bed was in a building that looked like a hospital, barn, bar combination. People would come and go, and different people would sit and talk with him. When Don wanted to respond, the angel would shake his head and touch his arm and said to him, "Not now."

As the dream progressed, the angel was always beside him when doctors and nurses walked in. At the foot of his bed was a cave-like opening that his bed could slide into. His son came to him trying to get him out of the place. His son was going to sneak him out of there, but before he could, the angel spoke to him and placed four butterflies on his face—two on his forehead, one on his cheek and one on his chin—and said he was given eternal life. Then he awoke and was in the hospital with his son beside him.

Don had asked many people to explain his dream to him, and nobody was able to make sense out of it for him. He wanted to know about the butterflies. The first day I met Don, he told me this dream. God spoke to me as Don shared with me. I told Don,

> "The butterflies represented eternal life. They are a symbol of resurrection. God gave you a gift and the assurance that you have eternal life. You don't need to be afraid. He gave to you an angel to walk the journey with you. When it comes time for you to let go of this world, God will probably send to you the angel to be with you."

Don said he sure hoped so because the angel gave him such peace.

The day before Don passed away, he began to see this angel. Don died in peace.

I had another hospice patient, Tom, who began to see a little boy angel in his home. He described him as young—about eight or nine years old, blonde and with a smile. Tom, an elderly man, would describe that he would come briefly and then leave. He was comforted by this angel, knowing God was with him.

This little boy angel seemed to follow me around with other patients in the same area who described seeing a little boy just like Pastor Judy and Tom saw. I believe this little angel boy was present with those who saw him, and that he brought great comfort and support to them.

My husband also had an angel that came to be with him. About three months after being diagnosed with brain tumors, Dave saw her sitting on the edge of our sofa in our home. He asked if I saw her and of course, I said no. After several times of seeing someone and asking if I had seen her, I realized it was an angel. Dave was able to describe her in detail—about thirteen or fourteen years old, a girl with blonde hair, a gap between her front teeth, wearing a blue blouse and as Dave called them, pantaloons. She did not say anything but would just sit for a moment, and then she would be gone. This angel came for several weeks, and Dave became very comfortable with her presence. Then she was gone for several months.

Dave wondered why. I believed that God sent her so Dave would be comfortable and familiar with her, and when it was his time to go to heaven she would return, and he would not be afraid. She would be with him and take him to heaven. Several weeks before Dave died, the angel returned briefly, bringing with her an elderly lady wearing a babushka, as Dave called it. Then the young girl angel would come daily and sit on the edge of his bed several times a day. The week of Dave's death the angel returned and lingered with Dave. Dave was comfortable with the angel and was less anxious and afraid.

Dave also experienced a glimpse of heaven. Once while in the hospital, Dave dreamed about heaven and saw the beauty of it but was unable to hear anything or go any further. It wasn't his time. Then two days before Dave died, he went into a coma-like state and saw heaven. After coming back and being able to talk, he described the beauty of heaven. Dave described the brilliant colors of everything he experienced. He talked about walking a path with intense green trees and meadows with bright colored flowers. It was vivid and bright. And then he said he could not describe all that he saw, that it was beyond description in words. He felt a complete peace and love that he had never experienced. He wanted to know when he could go back.

Through these and many other experiences with people who were dying and my own faith and understanding of the Bible, I believe heaven is real. I believe my loved ones are in heaven. I believe one day I will be reunited with them in heaven. This gives me great comfort and peace in the midst of my grief. It has helped me to accept their dying as a passage into the next life.

CHAPTER 23

MOURNING THE FUTURE

As you journey through your grief, you recognize that you grieve for what used to be. You remember the past and at times wish you could live there again. You remember with sadness and with joy mingled together. You remember the good times and the struggles. You look at pictures and remember spending time together and the adventures you had together.

You grieve the present with your feelings of being alone and sad, feeling the emptiness and void that your loved one leaves in your daily life. You try to do things you used to do, but it does not feel the same. You try to figure out how to live with this hole in your heart and to function through the day.

Some days you do well, and others days you feel as though you just survived or existed. You fall into bed exhausted but wonder what you did that day. Your grief makes you tired, but you try to go through the motions and the days in hopes you will feel better and move forward. You begin to recognize that the fog is lifting and the numbness is wearing off. Some days you feel something and wonder what it is. You laugh and smile and realize even in the midst of your grief, those moments are becoming good. You begin to see the beauty of the flowers, the white puffy clouds against the blue sky. You are becoming present in the moment. The grief still hurts, but you begin to believe that you can live and have a life.

Then you think of the future, and the grief becomes intense again. You have grieved the past and are grieving the present, but now you recognize a different grief. You begin to grieve the future. You think about life without your loved one, and it does not seem possible to make plans without your loved one. You think about taking a vacation or a trip and wonder how you will do that without your loved one.

In the loss of a child or grandchild, you grieve the future relationship. You grieve the loss of a shared relationship and what their life would have been. You grieve the events of life that your child or grandchild will never experience and that you will never have the opportunity to experience with them.

You grieve your plan and dream for the future. You had an idea of what life was going to be in the future. You had a plan, and your loved one was a vital part of the plan. Your dream is shattered. It does not seem possible to have another plan.

You grieve your vision of the future. You think about the future and what it looks like without your loved one. It does not seem possible, but you know that this next chapter of your life is beginning to unfold. It does not look like you thought it would, but you know God is already there in the future. God is preparing the road for you to walk into this new chapter and new adventure. Your loved one goes with you in your heart, and you take what you learned and how they made a difference in your life with you. Their love goes with you in your heart.

CHAPTER 24

OUR NEW REALITY

Our thoughts are getting clearer, and the reality that our loved one will no longer be physically present in our lives is beginning to become evident. The concept of "moving forward" feels as if we are letting go of our loved one and don't care anymore. Let us redefine what it means to move forward. It means to recognize the deep love and the meaning of our loved one's life and to take all that we learned and all that we are because of our loved one into the next chapter of our life.

Grief is a journey through mourning, sadness and uncertainty to find a new meaning and purpose to the life we have been given. Romans 8:28 tells us that God has something more for our lives: "We know that in everything God works for good with those who love him, who are called according to his purpose." (RSV) God will bring good out of the bad.

We are trying to find a way to re-engage in life. We celebrate the past and the legacy of our loved one and what we have learned because of that person in our lives. Our goal is to slowly establish a new normal, or what I prefer to call a new reality. A new normal says that life can become normal again. It is never normal without our loved one, but it does become real. It is our new reality.

This new reality is a process. Like a book, we begin a new chapter. While each chapter in a book is different but builds on the previous chapter, so it is with our lives. Each chapter is different, but we take the love and what we learned from previous chapters into the next one.

Our purpose in life does not necessarily change, just the way and with whom we live out the purpose may change. We are still in relationship with other people in our lives.

We realize we are different. What we liked in the past may not be what we enjoy now because we enjoyed it with our loved one. We learn to live and to laugh, but it is different. Different isn't bad; it is just different. Our perspective and priorities may change, and we have to re-evaluate what we are passionate about and what gives meaning to our lives. Our priorities may change because grief has guided us in seeing what is really important in life. Relationships and how we live in relationship with those we love become a priority. Life is precious and we realize it in our grief.

Don't rush this new reality. Be patient and wait. Nurture the growth within you and give it time to deepen its roots. Take time to ponder and wait. You will know when you are ready to slowly take the next steps into this new way of living and begin to live with acceptance and a purpose.

You may choose to continue the legacy of your loved one and choose a project in which to honor your loved one. You may begin to feel their love and become passionate about expressing it in some tangible way which gives a renewed purpose to your own life. You begin to put energy and love into a new experience and a new adventure.

Or your new reality may be a time of reflection and memories. You remember stories and share pictures with others to assist in helping the difference they made in your life and the life of others continue.

Your new reality may include major changes of relocating and developing a new home, or it may involve remaining where you are and being aware of the difference and coming to an acceptance.

Life is different, but it is still your life to be lived. The reality is that you allow your loved one to be physically gone, as you do, your heart recognizes that the love remains. You begin to remember, not with sadness but with a cherished love, the person, his/her life, the meaning and purpose of his/her life and the difference made in your life. Memories are transformed to a thankfulness, and you begin to smile in the remembrances.

"For I know the plans I have for you, says the Lord, plans for welfare and not for evil, to give you a future and a hope." (Jeremiah 29:11)

CHAPTER 25

THE FOUNDATION

As I sat in the pew at Wesley Chapel United Methodist Church, the church in which I spent the first eighteen years of my life, I realized I was surrounded by a great cloud of witnesses as Hebrews 12 describes — those who have gone before us. I could name the people and where they sat in the pews, but more importantly, their influence in my life.

I thought of my parents who brought me to church each Sunday and lived their faith daily. My grief for my parents has changed over the years. Yes, I miss them and wish I could still talk to them, but because of their lives and the foundation of faith, values, morals and life they gave me, I am who I am.

I recognized today there is a foundation of grief in our lives. I have been blessed with many people to give me guidance, direction and love on the path of life. Each person is like a stone in the foundation of who I am. Because they lived and because they died and are now in heaven, I recognize the difference they made in my life. I reflect on what I learned from our interactions and how they lived their lives. In the daily living with people and just living, I tend not to focus on the difference people make in my life and how they add to who I am. It is usually after a person has died we become reflective about their lives and their influence on us.

Each generation builds upon previous generations. To visualize this, think of your grandparents and great-grandparents and those before them as the foundation of your house. You may live, believe or have values based on the previous generations, and they have laid the foundation work for how you currently live, think, believe and work. It does not mean you do the same things or act the same way or even live in the same place, but they have influenced your current situation.

Therefore, as you grieve the loss of family, you recognize that they become part of the foundation of your house—your life. They become a part of who you are. As I pondered this thought, I have come to believe my parents and grandparents are part of the firm foundation of my life.

As I grieve the loss of my husband, I am beginning to understand that he is part of what I have built on the foundation. How we live and the relationships we have create the house upon our foundation. Some of the rooms are wide and open and are filled with memories while others are small and have very few pictures on the walls. But each is a part of who we have become.

I am who I am because I shared a love relationship. The love never ends, neither does the influence. They become a part of my house. We do not remove the room when they die but continue to build the house of our lives around their influence.

Sometimes we try to hold on to our loved one out of fear we will forget. We may go through a day and not think of them or feel sad, and then we feel guilty. I have come to accept that my husband lives within me—who he was and is continues to live on in me. He is a part of who I am. We do not think about the individual parts of our physical body each day, but that does not mean they are not a part of us. I am who I am because of the life and love we shared. He is an integral part of my day just like each body part is a vital and integral part of who I am.

CHAPTER 26

CELEBRATION OF LIFE LIVED

This chapter has taken the longest time to write because I have had to come to this reality in my own grief. I have had to experience the celebration of life before I can share how I have come to this place.

As I have accepted that my husband has died and is gone from this physical world, my relationship with him has deepened within me. I recognize the spiritual connection and who I am because we shared life together. My husband becomes a part of my spirit and soul. The love has nothing to do with action; that has been completed. It is a love now that connects within my heart.

Love is stronger than death. The intimacy with our loved one is in a different form. My love is more pure. I can no longer do anything for my husband but to love in the memories and remember his love for me. In the last anniversary card, he wrote these words: "You mean the world to me. My heart aches I love you so much." I understand heart ache and know that I will continue to survive and live in this deep love ache.

I will continue to tell the stories of his life—what I learned from him, how he made a difference in my life and in those around him, and I will give thanks for the blessing of being able to walk the path of life with him. I will always miss him and at times have tears and sadness. I give myself permission to have these moments. For Psalm 30:5 states, "Weeping may linger for the night, but joy comes with the morning." (NRSV) The night represents our grief, and the day represents our celebration of a life well lived. Other nights of sadness will come again, but we know the sadness will not last forever. A life of hope is ahead of us.

I have gained a deeper appreciation of the journey. My husband and I had separate paths in our lives. We came together to walk this path of life. He helped me move further along on my own life path, and then we came to a fork in the road. He took the path to heaven, and now I am to journey on this path in life. I realize I would not be as far along on my life journey if my husband had not come to walk beside me—to help me, strengthen me, love me and bring out the gifts in me. Therefore, I am able to celebrate his life, mourn his death and accept that he has made a difference in my life. He continues to journey with me in my heart. Nobody can ever take that love and spirit away.

I celebrate the lives of those who have enriched my life and made a difference in who I am. A little piece of each one of them is in my heart. As I recognize these gifts, my loved ones live on and bear fruit in my life and in the lives they have touched.

When I talk about my mom, share one of her recipes or share about her faith, I celebrate her life. I am sad she is not here, but I can celebrate now because a piece of her is in my heart. She continues to bear fruit in the lives of her family.

The journey of grief never ends; it just takes on different forms, and we learn to live in the midst of it. Grief and joy just become a part of who we are, and we are stronger and able to help others who follow us on this journey.

Memories of a life lived become a blessing. We remember and are thankful for the time shared together. We recognize the impact our loved one made on our lives and we are forever grateful.

Chapter 27

Anniversaries and Holidays

As we approach special days of our lives—birthdays, wedding anniversaries and holidays—our grief may intensify, and the idea of experiencing these special days without our loved one may seem impossible and overwhelming.

Admit that you will be sad, and the emotions will be heightened in these days. Expecting the emotional roller coaster helps to prepare you. Recognize your loved one's birthday. Your loved one was born and lived; celebrate the life lived. You will be sad, but you may want to do something in memory of your loved by giving thanks for the gift of life. There are many ideas: a balloon launch, flowers at the cemetery, a birthday cake with family, a memorial gift or assistance to an organization, or just being together with those you love.

The one special day that is usually overlooked and rarely talked about is your own birthday. Yes, the birthday of the one who is grieving is usually ignored as a sad day. If your loved one made your birthday special, always wrote you a card or gave you a special gift, the emptiness of your birthday is evident in your grief. My husband always wrote me a letter on my birthday. I have every letter/card he wrote me, and now I read them on my birthday so as to feel his loving presence.

If your spouse died, the wedding anniversary date reminds you that you are alone. The one you committed your life to is no longer present. Give yourself permission to be sad. Some may have had an anniversary tradition. My husband and I always would light our unity candle from our wedding service and say a prayer together thanking God for bringing us together and the deep love we had for one another. I continue to light the candle and to thank God for the gift of love. I go through pictures from our wedding and remember our life together. Sadness and loneliness mingle with joy and thanksgiving. I know that our love remains in my heart, and that love never dies.

Holidays with all their traditions are especially difficult in our grief journey. The difficulty is in figuring out how to maneuver through what is important—traditions, the needs of family and your own emotions. You want to remember your loved one even though it brings sadness. For Thanksgiving, many families have found it helpful to set a place at the table for the loved one—an empty chair. It becomes a living reminder that the loved one is still present in the midst of the family holiday meal.

Christmas seems to cause the most turmoil in our grief because of all the family traditions associated with the holiday and the emotion of the holiday itself. As you grieve, you may need to re-assess what you can do, what is most important, what you could let go of, and what you are really capable of experiencing emotionally.

Recognize that Christmas will not be the same no matter how you try to do everything the way you used to do. Your loved one is not present. Give yourself permission to celebrate Christmas differently—maybe just the first Christmas or maybe from now on. Choose what is important, and do not get lost in what you feel obligated to do. Talk with family about making some changes and how the family feels about Christmas traditions. Christmas will always be emotional no matter the years from the death of your loved ones. Christmas is rooted in love—the love God has for each of us by sending His son. Christmas is about love, so each year as we gather, we remember the love of those not with us.

Take some quiet time during the holidays to reflect and grieve. Do not totally isolate yourself from those you love. Accept invitations to Christmas dinners and events, but do not feel obligated to go everywhere. Make healthy choices for yourself.

For many people, the one-year anniversary of the death of a loved one is a very difficult time. You have survived an entire year without your loved one. It has been a struggle at times, but you have done something you did not think was possible. Remember with love your loved one.

Here are some ideas for handling the one-year anniversary:

- Spend the day with family or friends and share stories of your loved one.
- Reach out to others who are grieving and share together.
- Do something special to remember your loved one—light a candle, look at photo albums, release balloons or butterflies, plant a tree or flowers, place flowers on the grave, write a poem or say a prayer.
- Give a memorial gift in memory of your loved one.
- Create a memory box of things that remind you of your loved one—pictures, letters, awards, stories and memorabilia.
- Allow yourself to cry. Tears are a cleansing of the soul.

Each year when the anniversary date of death approaches, you will feel the loss and sadness. It may feel like it just happened all over again, and it *has* again in your heart, as you remember and grieve. Allow yourself time on this date to grieve and to be thankful for the gift of your loved one in your life.

> "Do not fear, for I am with you, do not be afraid, for I am your God; I will strengthen you, I will help you, I will uphold you with my victorious right hand." (Isaiah 41:10, NRSV)

CHAPTER 28

THE DIGNITY OF GRIEF

In hospice, the phrase "death with dignity" is used to express the need to allow a person to die with respect to their wishes and to provide peace and comfort. So where is the dignity in grief?

According to dictionary.com, dignity is defined as "worthiness, bearing conduct and speech indicative of self-respect."

When those around us do not understand our grief or why we continue to grieve, we may feel a lack of respect. We may begin to hide our grief inside and feel that it is not worth sharing with those around us.

Grief, death and loss are not talked about because it makes people uncomfortable. Most people do not know what to say or how to handle the emotions that come with grief, especially the pain and tears. The dignity of being able to openly express our grief does not happen much in our society. It is as though we have to hide it and feel bad about ourselves because we still hurt and feel the deep pain and loss.

The dignity needs to be restored to grief. Allow one another to grieve in whatever way is needed. Grief

The dignity needs to be restored to grief. Allow one another to grieve in whatever way is needed. Grief continues for as long as it needs to. Grieve as long as it does not become unhealthy or harmful to self or others.

In death with dignity, we allow people to make choices and even write them down. We document their final wishes. But in grief, it seems there is an expectation that we should all go through the stages and then be fine. Grief is not neat and orderly. Many times it is complicated, chaotic and messy. Death can be all these too, but there is an essence of planning and dignity that is part of the dying process.

The journey of dying and the journey of grief have common factors. There will always be some type of grief in death. There is the certainty that all will die even though we don't want to admit it or talk about it. There will be grief, but many try to deny it or avoid it.

Grief honors the deep love we had for our loved one. We mourn the loss of someone so dear and important in our life. We are thankful our loved one lived, and we celebrate the gift of life, but grief recognizes the pain, the loss, the change and the hole in our lives. There is dignity in our grief; it is the respect for life lived.

CHAPTER 29

GRIEF AT A DISTANCE

I received two phone calls within three days from two daughters notifying me of the death of their mothers. The first daughter told me that her mom, Frances, had died. Frances was in one of the churches I had served, and we kept in touch over the years through letters and phone calls. Her beautiful smile will always remain in my heart.

The second call was from the daughter of Shirley. I had met Shirley when I was around sixteen years old when she was the camp counselor at the church camp I attended. I thought Shirley was old then, but we connected that week and kept in touch by letters for the next forty years.

It was significant that two daughters took the time in the midst of their grief to call me. I was neither someone in the family circle nor even someone they knew personally, but I was someone they had heard about from their mothers.

The relationship I had with these two women according to most people would not have been considered close or worthy of a phone call upon death. Both women made a difference in my life through their encouragement, support and Christ-like love that assisted in my growth and faith development. We had remained connected spiritually.

As I grieve the loss of these two ladies, I have become aware that if I share about the loss with others, the response I will receive is "Oh, how did you know them?" The conversation will move to something else without a recognition of my loss and grief. The loss is not regarded as worthy of sympathy nor the recognition my grief.

How do we grieve the loss of acquaintances, friends and people we encounter in a chapter of our lives? We may feel guilty for our feelings of grief and loss because other people were closer to them.

I recognized this aspect of grief during the visitation hours for my husband. People shared stories with me about how he had made an impact in their lives. I could see in their eyes the tears and the loss of a friend and fellow trooper. They were grieving even though I did not know them personally. My grief was intense and deep because of my love relationship with my husband, but they also had grief because of their relationship with their friend.

Each life is precious, and at death each person should be grieved. Each person who has crossed our path of life, no matter the length of time, is significant. If we remember the person and recognize the impact or impression made upon our lives, then we grieve the loss and celebrate the life.

We may not have had contact with the person for years, but when we hear of his/her death, we recognize the loss and sadness that comes over us. We become aware that a little piece of us has died too. The person may have been a source of strength during a difficult time, or we walked with the person through the trials of his/her life. A moment in time connected a relationship, even if it was for a moment.

Take the time to grieve. Your grief will be different. When we grieve the loss of family and very close relationships, our grief will be more intense and painful. When we grieve the loss of people we have encountered on our life journey, we recognize the sadness and loss, but we are quicker to recognize the difference they made in our lives. We remember with fondness and usually can describe the relationship. Even though we may not have spent time with them recently or even if our relationship was distant, we recognize that the person made a difference in our lives. We grieve the loss of life, and we celebrate the gift of life.

For me, my faith reminds me that God placed that person on my path for a reason. In their death, I reflect on what I learned from them and how God allowed us to journey for a moment or a short period of time together. My faith also reminds me that I will see them again in heaven.

CHAPTER 30

CONCLUSION

You have journeyed through these words and through your own grief. The journey continues after you conclude this book. My prayer is that you have taken the needed time to pause, reflect, work through, remember and begin to live in the midst of your grief.

Your grief is your own. You have come to accept that it is messy, hard and painful, but now you recognize the love you have for your loved one never ends. Your memories bring tears and thanksgiving for a life lived. Sorrow and love mingle together.

Give yourself permission to continue the grieving and to accept that life is different and will always be different. There is no returning to a normal. Different is not bad, it is just different. Remember, grieving is a gradual process and it takes time. Grief is a chapter of your life. You have changed. Who you are and how you are in relationship with others has changed.

Our loved one is no longer physically present with us. Their memories and influence in our lives endure, and the love remains in our hearts. We bring the past and its memories into the present and learn from the experience and the relationship—how two lives intersected and walked the path of life for a period of time. We persevere through this chapter.

We embrace who we are in our grief and begin to look deep within our soul believing in who we were, who we are and who we will be. Grief changes us. It alters our dreams and plans for life. We recognize the next chapter is not how we planned it, but we still attempt to live into this next chapter of life.

We stay in our grief as long as we are healing, learning, accepting and finding the hope of a possible hope and life. Linger in the memories and the love, and allow this expression to penetrate your heart and life. Give it time to grow into a manifestation of you. You concede that you are different because of the grief, but as the clouds of grief begin to clear, you perceive the foundation of faith that has sustained you in the fog of grief. The idea of hope has seemed impossible in the depth of your grief, but it is becoming a possibility.

You have stayed through the brokenness, the pain and the heartache. You have named the emotions and accepted that they are a part of your journey. My prayer for you is a prayer of hope—a hope of a hope. May you find peace in the midst of the loss, hope in the emptiness and a foundation for your life in the brokenness.

The journey of grief never ends; it just takes a different form. The intensity lessens as we learn to live without our loved one. We accept the separation and have the faith that our loved one is in heaven—that is my hope. Grief and peace mingle together to become a part of who we are. We are stronger and able to help others on the journey of grief.

Grief honors the deep love we had for our loved one. There is dignity in our grief. It is the respect for a life lived.

Who do you want to be now? Who does God want you to be? Ponder this now on your journey. Allow the sorrow and love to mingle together. You have been blessed by love. The love remains forever within your heart. Live in the different.

APPENDICES

APPENDIX A

SCRIPTURES FOR REFLECTION

"Even though I walk through the valley of the shadow of death, I will fear no evil; for you are with me; your rod and your staff they comfort me." (Psalm 23:4, NIV)

"Remember that I commanded you to be strong and brave. Don't be afraid, because the Lord your God will be with you everywhere you go." (Joshua 1:9, NCV)

"So, don't worry, because I am with you. Don't be afraid, because I am your God. I will make you strong and will help you; I will support you with my right hand that saves you." (Isaiah 41:10, NCV)

"The joy of the Lord is your strength." (Nehemiah 8:10, RSV)

"I lift up my eyes to the hills. From whence does my help come? My help comes from the Lord, who made heaven and earth." (Psalm 121:1-2, RSV)

"I can do all things through Christ who strengthens me." (Philippians 4:13, RSV)

"Fear not, for I have redeemed you; I have called you by name, you are mine. When you pass through the waters I will be with you; and through the rivers; they shall not overwhelm you; when you walk through fire you shall not be burned, and the flame shall not consume you." (Isaiah 43:1-2, RSV)

"God gives power to the faint and strengthens the powerless. Those who wait for the Lord shall renew their strength, they shall mount up with wings like eagles, they shall run and not be weary, they shall walk and not faint." (Isaiah 40:29, 31, NRSV)

"But I will call to God, and the Lord saves me. Evening, morning and noon I cry out in distress, and he hears my voice. (Psalm 55:16-17, NIV)

"The Lord is my strength, He makes me like a deer that does not stumble so I can walk on the steep mountains." (Habakkuk 3:19, NCV)

"Come to me, all you that are weary and are carrying heaven burdens, and I will give you rest." (Matthew 11:28, NRSV)

"Let us therefore come boldly unto the throne of grace, that we may obtain mercy, and find grace to help in time of need." (Hebrews 4:16, KJV)

"He comforts us every time we have trouble, so when others have trouble, we can comfort them with the same comfort God give us." (2 Corinthians 1:4, NCV)

"Commit thy way unto the Lord, trust also in him; and he shall bring it to pass." (Psalm 37:5, KJV)

"Do not worry about anything, but pray and ask God for everything you need, always giving thanks." (Philippians 4:6, NCV)

"Be joyful always; pray continually; give thanks in all circumstances, for this is God's will for you in Christ Jesus." (Thessalonians 5:16-18, NIV)

"Jesus said, "I am the resurrection and the life. Those who believe in me will have life even if they die. And everyone who lives and believes in me will never die." (John 11:25-26, NCV)

"For I know the plans I have for you, says the Lord, plans for welfare and not for evil, to give you a future and a hope. Then you will call upon me and come and pray to me, and I will hear you. You will seek me and find me; when you seek me with all your heart." (Jeremiah 29:11-13, RSV)

"Humble yourselves therefore under the mighty hand of God, that in due time he may exalt you. Cast all your anxieties on him, for he cares about you." (1 Peter 5:6-7, RSV)

"I have fought the good fight. I have finished the race. I have kept the faith." (Timothy 4:7, RSV)

BENEDICTIONS

"May our Lord Jesus Christ himself and God our Father encourage you and strengthen you in every good thing you do and say. God loves us, and through his grace he gave us a good hope and encouragement that continues forever." (2 Thessalonians 2:16-17, NCV)

"May the Lord make your love grow more and multiply for each other and for all people so that you will love others as we love you. May your hearts be made strong so that you will be holy and without fault before our God and Father when our Lord Jesus comes with all his holy ones." (I Thessalonians 3:12-13, NCV)

"May the Lord bless you and keep you. May the Lord show you his kindness and have mercy on you. May the Lord watch over you and give you peace." (Numbers 6:24-26, NCV)

"I pray that the God who gives hope will fill you with much joy and peace while you trust in him. Then your hope will overflow by the power of the Holy Spirit." (Romans 15:13, NCV)

"And God's peace, which is so great we cannot understand it, will keep your hearts and minds in Christ Jesus." (Philippians 4:7, NCV)

"I am sure that neither death, nor life, nor angels, nor ruling spirits, nothing now, nothing in the future, no powers, nothing above us, nothing below us, nor anything else in the whole world will ever be able to separate us from the love of God that is in Christ Jesus our Lord." (Romans 8:38-39, NCV)

Made in the USA
Columbia, SC
02 July 2018